wor

GW00507929

worldscapes

A collection of verse compiled by
Robin Malan

Cape Town • OXFORD UNIVERSITY PRESS • 1997

Oxford University Press

Walton Street, Oxford ox2 6DP, United Kingdom

Oxford, New York,
Athens, Bangkok, Calcutta, Cape Town, Chennai, Dar es Salaam, Delhi,
Florence, Hong Kong, Istanbul, Karachi, Kuala Lumpur, Madrid,
Melbourne, Mexico City, Mumbai, Nairobi, Paris, Singapore, Taipei,
Tokyo, Toronto

and associated companies in
Berlin, Ibadan

Oxford is a trade mark of Oxford University Press

Worldscapes

ISBN 0 19 574571 1
© Oxford University Press 1997

COMMISSIONING EDITOR: Daphne Paizee
EDITOR: Sharon Hughes
DESIGNER: Peter Burgess
COVER PHOTO: Image Bank

Published by Oxford University Press Southern Africa
PO Box 12119, N1 City, 7463, Cape Town, South Africa

Set in Minion & Avenir by RHT desktop publishing cc
Cover reproduction by RJH Graphic Reproduction
Printed by Creda Press Epping

Contents

in chronological order of authors

1940–49

Introduction

It is almost thirty years since *Inscapes* first appeared, and it is ten years since *New Inscapes* was published. What should *Worldscapes*, this new revision, this anthology for the end of the 1990s and the start of the twenty-first century, look like and be about?

One of the first issues to be dealt with is 'the canon', the 'representative overview of English poetry in periods and movements', starting with a bit of Chaucer, some Shakespeare sonnets…etc. It was only twenty years ago, when I first started teaching in an international educational framework, that I realized that there is no Universal Diktat that the canon be prescribed, taught and studied. I discovered there was another world. One year it would be only Robert Frost's poetry that was prescribed. Another year students would carry around two slim volumes: Philip Larkin's *The Less Deceived* and Robert Lowell's *Life Studies*. A third year it would be poems by three poets: the American Denise Levertov, the South African Mongane Wally Serote and the Nigerian Gabriel Okara. I discovered that in some quarters it was thought that the proper realm of the canon was university studies and that it had no place in the secondary school. In any event, teaching some of the 'classical poems' became an extra-curricular enjoyment you took your students into occasionally when the 'pressures' of the syllabus allowed.

I have, however, kept the canon – or, at least, enough of it to make the representative or historical approach perfectly possible. Apart from adding a few less-anthologized Shakespeare sonnets, I have not tried to find 'new', 'different', 'other' poems by the major figures. I am aware of the argument that some teachers say they get tired of teaching the same poems. On the other hand, when I pick up an anthology, I am simply irritated if I can't find the major poems of the major poets but find lesser works instead. And I certainly don't want to spend time teaching the lesser when I could be handling the more important poems.

Of far greater concern to me has been that the anthology might serve to open up students' experience. By this I mean their experience of English as much as their world view. We need to be aware that there is a world out there. We need to know that English is a language written and spoken by many different sorts of people. I have therefore thought it important to cast the selection-net wide. I have not included works translated from other languages, but I have included poems that are distinctively African, African American, American, Australian, British, Canadian, Caribbean, Indian, Pakistani, South African, and West Indian-British (to mention them alphabetically). Together they make up an excitingly varied experience of life and of the ways English is currently being used.

In all of this I have been keen to make an anthology that serves more than the purpose of examination prescription. I want this to be a book that teachers will read on their own, that students will read on their own, and that teachers and students will use in class for reasons unrelated to exams or prescriptions. Just because the poems interest, intrigue and excite them.

RM
Cape Town
1997

the poems

Geoffrey Chaucer (*c* 1343–1400)

Chaucer served in Edward III's invading army in France; went abroad on various diplomatic missions, and was appointed controller of customs in London. In *The Canterbury Tales* he gives a broad picture of English life by having a group of pilgrims tell stories on their way to Canterbury to pay homage to Saint Thomas à Becket, who was murdered there in 1170.

This extract from the Introduction to the Prologue is given in its original Middle English. Try reading it aloud and then translating it. Read it giving each sound its full value, for example in 'droghte' (line 2) the 'gh' is the guttural sound you find in Afrikaans and the Nguni languages.

The extract tells how April and its 'sweet showers' break the 'drought' of March (remember, Chaucer lived in the northern hemisphere, and so these are light spring rains), cause the young plants (the 'tendre croppes') to grow and the birds (the 'smale foweles') to sing. It's then that people feel the urge to go on pilgrimages. At the Tabard Inn in Southwark, in the south of London, the poet meets up with twenty-nine pilgrims bound for Canterbury, gets to know them, and joins them.

From the Prologue to *The Canterbury Tales*
Introduction

Whan that Aprill with his shoures soote
The droghte of March hath perced to the roote,
And bathed every veyne in swich licour
Of which vertu engendred is the flour;
Whan Zephirus eek with his sweete breeth
Inspired hath in every holt and heeth
The tendre croppes, and the yonge sonne
Hath in the Ram his halve cours yronne,
And smale foweles maken melodye,
That slepen al the nyght with open ye
(So priketh hem nature in hir corages);
Thanne longen folk to goon on pilgrimages,
And palmeres for to seken straunge strondes,
To ferne halwes, kowthe in sondry londes;
And specially from every shires ende
Of Engelond to Caunterbury they wende,
The hooly blisful martir for to seke,
That hem hath holpen whan that they were seeke.
Bifil that in that seson on a day,
In Southwerk at the Tabard as I lay
Redy to wenden on my pilgrymage

To Caunterbury with ful devout corage,
At nyght was come into that hostelrye
Wel nyne and twenty in a compaignye,
Of sondry folk, by aventure yfalle
In felaweshipe, and pilgrimes were they alle,
That toward Caunterbury wolden ryde.
The chambres and the stables weren wyde,
And wel we weren esed atte beste.
And shortly, whan the sonne was to reste,
So hadde I spoken with hem everichon
That I was of hir felaweshipe anon,
And made forward erly for to ryse,
To take oure wey ther as I yow devyse.
   But nathelees, whil I have tyme and space,
Er that I ferther in this tale pace,
Me thynketh it acordaunt to resoun
To telle yow al the condicioun
Of ech of hem, so as it semed me,
And whiche they weren, and of what degree.

From the Prologue to *The Canterbury Tales*
The Wife of Bath

(translated by Nevill Coghill)

A worthy woman from beside Bath city
Was with us, somewhat deaf, which was a pity.
In making cloth she showed so great a bent
She bettered those of Ypres and of Ghent.
In all the parish not a dame dared stir
Towards the altar steps in front of her,
And if indeed they did, so wrath was she
As to be quite put out of charity.
Her kerchiefs were of finely woven ground;
I dared have sworn they weighed a good ten pound,
The ones she wore on Sunday, on her head.
Her hose were of the finest scarlet red
And gartered tight; her shoes were soft and new.
Bold was her face, handsome, and red in hue.
A worthy woman all her life, what's more
She'd had five husbands, all at the church door,

Apart from other company in youth;
No need just now to speak of that, forsooth.
And she had thrice been to Jerusalem,
Seen many strange rivers and passed over them;
She'd been to Rome and also to Boulogne,
St James of Compostella and Cologne,
And she was skilled in wandering by the way.
She had gap-teeth, set widely, truth to say.
Easily on an ambling horse she sat
Well wimpled up, and on her head a hat
As broad as is a buckler or a shield;
She had a flowing mantle that concealed
Large hips, her heels spurred sharply under that.
In company she liked to laugh and chat
And knew the remedies for love's mischances,
An art in which she knew the oldest dances.

Christopher (Kit) Marlowe (1564–1593)

Marlowe, born in Canterbury, seems to have led a life full of adventure, such as being deported from the Netherlands for attempting to issue forged gold coins. He wrote a number of popular plays. He was killed in a tavern brawl.

The passionate shepherd to his love

Come live with me and be my love,
And we will all the pleasures prove,
That hills and valleys, dales and fields,
And all the craggy mountains yields.

There we will sit upon the rocks,
And see the shepherds feed their flocks,
By shallow rivers to whose falls
Melodious birds sing madrigals.

And I will make thee beds of roses
With a thousand fragrant posies,
A cap of flowers, and a kirtle
Embroidered all with leaves of myrtle;

A gown made of the finest wool
Which from our pretty lambs we pull;

Fair lined slippers for the cold,
With buckles of the purest gold;

A belt of straw and ivy buds,
With coral clasps and amber studs:
And if these pleasures may thee move,
Come live with me and be my love.

The shepherds' swains shall dance and sing
For thy delight each May morning:
If these delights thy mind may move,
Then live with me and be my love.

Sir Walter Ralegh (1552–1618)

Ralegh was an explorer, navigator and colonizer. After Elizabeth I's death he was
imprisoned in the Tower of London, then released to search for gold he claimed
to have discovered in Guyana twenty years before. On his return (without the
gold) he was tried for treason and executed.

The nymph's reply to the shepherd

If all the world and love were young,
And truth in every shepherd's tongue,
These pretty pleasures might me move
To live with thee and be thy love.

Time drives the flocks from field to fold,
When rivers rage and rocks grow cold,
And Philomel becometh dumb;
The rest complain of cares to come.

The flowers do fade, and wanton fields
To wayward winter reckoning yields;
A honey tongue, a heart of gall,
Is fancy's spring, but sorrow's fall.

Thy gowns, thy shoes, thy beds of roses,
Thy cap, thy kirtle, and thy posies
Soon break, soon wither, soon forgotten,
In folly ripe, in reason rotten.

Thy belt of straw and ivy buds,
Thy coral clasps and amber studs,
All these in me no means can move
To come to thee and be thy love.

But could youth last and love still breed,
Had joys no date nor age no need,
Then these delights my mind might move
To live with thee and be thy love.

William Shakespeare (1564–1616)

Shakespeare was born, educated and married in the Warwickshire country town of Stratford. At some point he left his family there and went to work in the theatre in London. Apart from writing 36 plays, he wrote a few long poems, and a sequence of 154 sonnets, which reflect both his affection for a young man of rank and beauty (sonnets 1 to 126) and his love for the mysterious 'dark lady' of the sonnets (sonnets 127 to 154). When the sonnets were published in 1609, they were dedicated 'To the onlie begetter of these insuing sonnets, Mr W. H.' Much ingenious literary detective work has been done for nearly four centuries to try to find out who Mr W. H. was.

The sonnet rhyme-scheme *abab cdcd efef gg* was the one favoured by Shakespeare, and so is called either the Elizabethan sonnet or the Shakespearean sonnet.

Sonnet 29
When in disgrace with fortune and men's eyes

When in disgrace with fortune and men's eyes,
I all alone beweep my outcast state,
And trouble deaf heaven with my bootless cries,
And look upon myself and curse my fate,
Wishing me like to one more rich in hope,
Featured like him, like him with friends possessed,
Desiring this man's art, and that man's scope,
With what I most enjoy contented least;
Yet in these thoughts myself almost despising,
Haply I think on thee, and then my state,
Like to the lark at break of day arising
From sullen earth, sings hymns at heaven's gate;
    For thy sweet love remembered such wealth brings
    That then I scorn to change my state with kings.

Sonnet 71

No longer mourn for me when I am dead

No longer mourn for me when I am dead
Than you shall hear the surly sullen bell
Give warning to the world that I am fled
From this vile world with vilest worms to dwell.
Nay, if you read this line, remember not
The hand that writ it, for I love you so
That I in your sweet thoughts would be forgot,
If thinking on me then should make you woe.
O if (I say) you look upon this verse,
When I (perhaps) compounded am with clay,
Do not so much as my poor name rehearse;
But let your love even with my life decay,
    Lest the wise world should look into your moan,
    And mock you with me after I am gone.

Sonnet 104

To me, fair friend, you never can be old

To me, fair friend, you never can be old,
For as you were when first your eye I eyed,
Such seems your beauty still. Three winters cold
Have from the forests shook three summers' pride,
Three beauteous springs to yellow autumn turned
In process of the seasons have I seen,
Three April perfumes in three hot Junes burned
Since first I saw you fresh, which yet are green.
Ah yet doth beauty, like a dial hand,
Steal from his figure, and no pace perceived,
So your sweet hue, which methinks still doth stand,
Hath motion, and mine eye may be deceived.
    For fear of which, hear this, thou age unbred:
    Ere you were born was beauty's summer dead.

Sonnet 116

Let me not to the marriage of true minds

Let me not to the marriage of true minds
Admit impediments. Love is not love

Which alters when it alteration finds,
Or bends with the remover to remove.
O, no, it is an ever-fixèd mark
That looks on tempests and is never shaken;
It is the star to every wand'ring bark,
Whose worth's unknown, although his height be taken.
Love's not Time's fool, though rosy lips and cheeks
Within his bending sickle's compass come;
Love alters not with his brief hours and weeks,
But bears it out even to the edge of doom.
    If this be error and upon me proved,
    I never writ, nor no man ever loved.

John Donne (1572–1631)

After some naval adventures and a brief imprisonment, Donne entered the church and eventually became the Dean of St Paul's Cathedral in London. He is equally well known for his religious poems as for his earlier love-poems.

Notice the unexpected scientific references in this love-poem; and the power and confidence of his religious faith in the famous sonnet that follows. 'Valediction' means saying goodbye.

bidding farewell

A valediction: forbidding mourning

As virtuous men pass mildly away,
    And whisper to their souls, to go,
Whilst some of their sad friends do say,
    The breath goes now, and some say, no:

So let us melt, and make no noise,
    No tear-floods, nor sigh-tempests move. *violate/pollute*
'Twere profanation of our joys
    To tell the laity our love. *non expert – profession/religion*

treat sacred thing with irreverance or disregard.

Moving of th' earth brings harms and fears,
    Men reckon what it did and meant.
But trepidation of the spheres, *fear/alarm/*
    Though greater far, is innocent. *tremulous agitation*

Dull sublunary lovers' love
    (Whose soul is sense) cannot admit
Absence, because it doth remove
    Those things which elemented it.

But we by a love, so much refined,
    That our selves know not what it is,
Inter-assurèd of the mind,
    Care less, eyes, lips, and hands to miss.

Our two souls therefore, which are one,
    Though I must go, endure not yet
A breach, but an expansion,
    Like gold to airy thinness beat.

If they be two, they are two so
    As stiff twin compasses are two,
Thy soul the fixed foot, makes no show
    To move, but doth, if th' other do.

And though it in the centre sit,
    Yet when the other far doth roam,
It leans, and hearkens after it,
    And grows erect, as that comes home.

Such wilt thou be to me, who must
    Like th' other foot, obliquely run;
Thy firmness draws my circle just,
    And makes me end, where I begun.

Death be not proud

Death be not proud, though some have called thee
Mighty and dreadful, for thou art not so,
For those, whom thou think'st thou dost overthrow,
Die not, poor death, nor yet canst thou kill me.
From rest and sleep, which but thy pictures be,
Much pleasure, then from thee much more must flow,
And soonest our best men with thee do go,
Rest of their bones, and souls' delivery.
Thou art slave to Fate, Chance, kings, and desperate men,
And dost with poison, war, and sickness dwell.
And poppy or charms can make us sleep as well,
And better than thy stroke; why swell'st thou then?
One short sleep past, we wake eternally,
And death shall be no more; death, thou shalt die.

John Milton (1608–74)

Milton supported Oliver Cromwell's republic after the execution of King Charles I in 1649, and was appointed Secretary of the Council of State. After the collapse of the republic and the restoration of Charles II in 1660 he was briefly imprisoned. He married three times, his first and second wives dying, the third surviving him. At the age of 35 he became aware that he was losing his eyesight; by the age of 44 he was completely blind.

On his blindness

When I consider how my light is spent,
Ere half my days, in this dark world and wide,
And that one Talent which is death to hide,
Lodged with me useless, though my Soul more bent
To serve therewith my Maker, and present
My true account, lest He returning chide,
'Doth God exact day-labour, light denied?'
I fondly ask. But Patience, to prevent
That murmur, soon replies, 'God doth not need
Either man's work or his own gifts. Who best
Bear his mild yoke, they serve him best. His State
Is Kingly: thousands at his bidding speed
And post o'er Land and Ocean without rest;
They also serve who only stand and wait.'

Andrew Marvell (1621–78)

Marvell was, at different times in his life, tutor to Oliver Cromwell's ward, Secretary to Cromwell's Council of State, a Member of Parliament, and, possibly, a spy.

To his coy mistress

Had we but world enough, and time,
This coyness, Lady, were no crime.
We would sit down and think which way
To walk, and pass our long love's day.
Thou by the Indian Ganges' side
Shouldst rubies find; I by the tide
Of Humber would complain. I would
Love you ten years before the Flood,

And you should, if you please, refuse
Till the conversion of the Jews.
My vegetable love should grow
Vaster than empires, and more slow.
An hundred years should go to praise
Thine eyes, and on thy forehead gaze.
Two hundred to adore each breast,
But thirty thousand to the rest.
An age at least to every part,
And the last age should show your heart.
For, Lady, you deserve this state,
Nor would I love at lower rate.

But at my back I always hear
Time's wingèd chariot hurrying near;
And yonder all before us lie
Deserts of vast eternity.
Thy beauty shall no more be found,
Nor, in thy marble vault, shall sound
My echoing song; then worms shall try
That long preserv'd virginity,
And your quaint honour turn to dust,
And into ashes all my lust:
The grave's a fine and private place,
But none, I think, do there embrace.

Now therefore, while the youthful hue
Sits on thy skin like morning dew,
And while thy willing soul transpires
At every pore with instant fires,
Now let us sport us while we may,
And now, like amorous birds of prey,
Rather at once our time devour,
Than languish in his slow-chapt power.
Let us roll all our strength and all
Our sweetness up into one ball,
And tear our pleasures with rough strife
Thorough the iron gates of life.
Thus, though we cannot make our sun
Stand still, yet we will make him run.

William Wordsworth (1770–1850)

Wordsworth was the acknowledged leader of what we call the Romantic movement (see also Coleridge (p. 12), Shelley (p. 13) and Keats (p. 14)). In his youth he was greatly inspired by the ideals of the French Revolution (he visited France in 1795); but then was sadly disillusioned by the excesses after the revolution. Equally, he set himself against the effects of the 'industrial revolution' in England.

Composed upon Westminster Bridge

Earth has not anything to show more fair:
Dull would he be of soul who could pass by
A sight so touching in its majesty:
This City now doth, like a garment, wear
The beauty of the morning: silent, bare
Ships, towers, domes, theatres, and temples lie
Open unto the fields, and to the sky;
All bright and glittering in the smokeless air.
Never did sun more beautifully steep
In his first splendour, valley, rock, or hill;
Ne'er saw I, never felt, a calm so deep!
The river glideth at his own sweet will:
Dear God! the very houses seem asleep;
And all that mighty heart is lying still!

The world is too much with us

The world is too much with us; late and soon,
Getting and spending, we lay waste our powers:
Little we see in Nature that is ours;
We have given our hearts away, a sordid boon!
This Sea that bares her bosom to the moon;
The winds that will be howling at all hours,
And are up-gathered now like sleeping flowers;
For this, for everything, we are out of tune;
It moves us not. – Great God! I'd rather be
A Pagan suckled in a creed outworn;
So might I, standing on this pleasant lea,
Have glimpses that would make me less forlorn;
Have sight of Proteus rising from the sea;
Or hear old Triton blow his wreathèd horn.

Samuel Taylor Coleridge (1772–1834)

Coleridge embarked on a brilliant career at Cambridge University, but was distracted by French revolutionary politics, heavy drinking and an unhappy love affair. Later he married, and formed a long and fruitful literary friendship with William Wordsworth and his sister Dorothy. They eventually quarrelled and broke off all contact.

He took opium, to which he eventually became addicted. On one occasion when he had taken opium and fallen asleep, he had a 'vision' and composed a long poem in his mind. After waking, he was writing down what he had composed, when he was famously interrupted by 'a person from Porlock', after which he could recall nothing. This fragment is all that remained.

Kubla Khan

In Xanadu did Kubla Khan
A stately pleasure-dome decree:
Where Alph, the sacred river, ran
Through caverns measureless to man
    Down to a sunless sea.
So twice five miles of fertile ground
With walls and towers were girdled round:
And there were gardens bright with sinuous rills,
Where blossomed many an incense-bearing tree;
And here were forests ancient as the hills,
Enfolding sunny spots of greenery.

But oh! that deep romantic chasm which slanted
Down the green hill athwart a cedarn cover!
A savage place! as holy and enchanted
As e'er beneath a waning moon was haunted
By woman wailing for her demon-lover!
And from this chasm, with ceaseless turmoil seething,
As if this earth in fast thick pants were breathing,
A mighty fountain momently was forced:
Amid whose swift half-intermitted burst
Huge fragments vaulted like rebounding hail,
Or chaffy grain beneath the thresher's flail:
And 'mid these dancing rocks at once and ever
It flung up momently the sacred river.
Five miles meandering with a mazy motion
Through wood and dale the sacred river ran,
Then reached the caverns measureless to man,

And sank in tumult to a lifeless ocean:
And 'mid this tumult Kubla heard from far
Ancestral voices prophesying war!

    The shadow of the dome of pleasure
    Floated midway on the waves;
    Where was heard the mingled measure
    From the fountain and the caves.
It was a miracle of rare device,
A sunny pleasure-dome with caves of ice!

    A damsel with a dulcimer
    In a vision once I saw:
    It was an Abyssinian maid,
    And on her dulcimer she played,
    Singing of Mount Abora.
    Could I revive within me
    Her symphony and song,
    To such a deep delight 'twould win me,
That with music loud and long,
I would build that dome in air,
That sunny dome! those caves of ice!
And all who heard should see them there,
And all should cry, Beware! Beware!
His flashing eyes, his floating hair!
Weave a circle round him thrice,
And close your eyes with holy dread,
For he on honey-dew hath fed,
And drunk the milk of Paradise.

Percy Bysshe Shelley (1792–1822)

Shelley was the son of an English baronet. He was educated at Eton, then
expelled from Oxford University (for circulating a pamphlet advocating
atheism). At the age of 19 he eloped with Harriet Westbrook; at the age of 22 he
eloped with Mary Wollstonecraft Godwin. Two years later Harriet committed
suicide by drowning, and Mary and Shelley married. Mary Shelley was the
author of the novel *Frankenstein*. The Shelleys settled in Italy. In 1822 Shelley and
a friend were drowned in a storm; the bodies were washed ashore some days
later. Shelley's body was ceremoniously burned on a funeral pyre on the beach
and the ashes buried in Rome.

    In 1817 Shelley had visited the British Museum to view the newly-acquired
Egyptian Rosetta Stone and the statue of Rameses II (sometimes called

Ozymandias). This visit inspired the following sonnet on the nature and fate of tyranny.

Ozymandias

I met a traveller from an antique land
Who said: Two vast and trunkless legs of stone
Stand in the desert ... Near them, on the sand,
Half sunk, a shattered visage lies, whose frown,
And wrinkled lip, and sneer of cold command,
Tell that its sculptor well those passions read
Which yet survive, stamped on these lifeless things,
The hand that mocked them, and the heart that fed:
And on the pedestal these words appear:
'My name is Ozymandias, king of kings:
Look on my works, ye Mighty, and despair!'
Nothing beside remains. Round the decay
Of that colossal wreck, boundless and bare
The lone and level sands stretch far away.

John Keats (1795–1821)

Keats was born in London (he was sometimes called 'the Cockney Poet'). He had a difficult life, having to look after his two younger brothers and his sister from the age of 14. He studied medicine, though he never practised. He nursed both his mother and his brother Tom through their fatal illnesses, and then himself also contracted tuberculosis. After three books of his poems were published (when he was 21, 22, and 24), he travelled to Italy in a vain attempt to regain his health. He died there at the age of 25. For the last two years of his life he was desperately in love with Fanny Brawne. They were unofficially engaged, and she nursed him for some weeks before he left England.

The 'fair creature' in this sonnet is not Fanny Brawne (whom he had not yet met), but an unknown young woman Keats saw one day in a park. He never got to know who she was, but she clearly made a strong impression on him. His burning ambition to become a poet is seen in the poem.

When I have fears

When I have fears that I may cease to be
   Before my pen has gleaned my teeming brain,
Before high-pilèd books, in charactery,
   Hold like rich garners the full ripened grain;

When I behold, upon the night's starred face,
    Huge cloudy symbols of a high romance,
And think that I may never live to trace
    Their shadows, with the magic hand of chance;
And when I feel, fair creature of an hour,
    That I shall never look upon thee more,
Never have relish in the faery power
    Of unreflecting love; – then on the shore
Of the wide world I stand alone, and think
Till love and fame to nothingness do sink.

Keats wrote four great odes (formal poems celebrating, and often addressed to, their subject) during 1818-19. He had recently visited the British Museum and seen the ancient Greek artefacts there (including the recently-acquired 'Elgin Marbles', marble statuary from the fifth century BC). He became fascinated by the idea that art depicts spontaneous liveliness yet is itself fixed, unchanging and permanent. Here his subject is the wedding scene painted around a Greek vase. 'Brede' in the fifth stanza means 'pattern'.

Ode on a Grecian urn

1

Thou still unravished bride of quietness,
    Thou foster-child of silence and slow time,
Sylvan historian, who canst thus express
    A flowery tale more sweetly than our rhyme:
What leaf-fringed legend haunts about thy shape
    Of deities or mortals, or of both,
        In Tempe or the dales of Arcady?
What men or gods are these? What maidens loth?
    What mad pursuit? What struggle to escape?
        What pipes and timbrels? What wild ecstasy?

2

Heard melodies are sweet, but those unheard
    Are sweeter; therefore, ye soft pipes, play on;
Not to the sensual ear, but, more endeared,
    Pipe to the spirit ditties of no tone:
Fair youth, beneath the trees, thou canst not leave
    Thy song, nor ever can those trees be bare;
        Bold Lover, never, never canst thou kiss,

Though winning near the goal – yet, do not grieve;
 She cannot fade, though thou hast not thy bliss,
  For ever wilt thou love, and she be fair!

3

Ah, happy, happy boughs! that cannot shed
 Your leaves, nor ever bid the Spring adieu;
And, happy melodist, unwearièd,
 For ever piping songs for ever new;
More happy love! more happy, happy love!
 For ever warm and still to be enjoyed,
  For ever panting, and for ever young;
All breathing human passion far above,
 That leaves a heart high-sorrowful and cloyed,
  A burning forehead, and a parching tongue.

4

Who are these coming to the sacrifice?
 To what green altar, O mysterious priest,
Lead'st thou that heifer lowing at the skies,
 And all her silken flanks with garlands drest?
What little town by river or sea-shore,
 Or mountain-built with peaceful citadel,
  Is emptied of its folk, this pious morn?
And, little town, thy streets for evermore
 Will silent be; and not a soul to tell
  Why thou art desolate can e'er return.

5

O Attic shape! Fair attitude! with brede
 Of marble men and maidens overwrought,
With forest branches and the trodden weed;
 Thou, silent form, dost tease us out of thought
As doth eternity: Cold Pastoral!
 When old age shall this generation waste,
  Thou shalt remain, in midst of other woe
Than ours, a friend to man, to whom thou say'st,
 Beauty is truth, truth beauty, – that is all
  Ye know on earth, and all ye need to know.

Lord Alfred Tennyson (1809–92)

Tennyson was born in Lincolnshire, and started writing poetry at the age of five. When he was 18 he entered Trinity College, Cambridge, and formed a very close friendship with Arthur Hallam, a brilliant young literary critic. Six years later he was devastated when Hallam died suddenly. Tennyson was engaged to Emily Sellwood for nineteen years, marrying her only after he had completed and published a sequence of elegies for Hallam. He named his first son Hallam. The literary historians Lionel Trilling and Harold Bloom said: 'His life had one event only, and that was the terrible experience of losing Hallam.' Tennyson was Britain's Poet Laureate (which means he was required to write poems for state occasions), and is buried in Westminster Abbey.

Ulysses

It little profits that an idle king,
By this still hearth, among these barren crags,
Matched with an agèd wife, I mete and dole
Unequal laws unto a savage race,
That hoard, and sleep, and feed, and know not me.
I cannot rest from travel: I will drink
Life to the lees: all times I have enjoyed
Greatly, have suffered greatly, both with those
That loved me, and alone; on shore, and when
Through scudding drifts the rainy Hyades
Vext the dim sea: I am become a name;
For always roaming with a hungry heart
Much have I seen and known; cities of men
And manners, climates, councils, governments,
Myself not least, but honoured of them all;
And drunk delight of battle with my peers,
Far on the ringing plains of windy Troy.
I am a part of all that I have met;
Yet all experience is an arch wherethrough
Gleams that untravelled world, whose margin fades
For ever and for ever when I move.
How dull it is to pause, to make an end,
To rust unburnished, not to shine in use!
As though to breathe were life. Life piled on life
Were all too little, and of one to me
Little remains: but every hour is saved
From that eternal silence, something more,

A bringer of new things; and vile it were
For some three suns to store and hoard myself,
And this grey spirit yearning in desire
To follow knowledge like a sinking star,
Beyond the utmost bound of human thought.

This is my son, mine own Telemachus,
To whom I leave the sceptre and the isle –
Well-loved of me, discerning to fulfil
This labour, by slow prudence to make mild
A rugged people, and through soft degrees
Subdue them to the useful and the good.
Most blameless is he, centred in the sphere
Of common duties, decent not to fail
In offices of tenderness, and pay
Meet adoration to my household gods,
When I am gone. He works his work, I mine.

There lies the port: the vessel puffs her sail:
There gloom the dark broad seas. My mariners,
Souls that have toiled, and wrought, and thought with me –
That ever with a frolic welcome took
The thunder and the sunshine, and opposed
Free hearts, free foreheads – you and I are old;
Old age hath yet his honour and his toil;
Death closes all: but something ere the end,
Some work of noble note may yet be done,
Not unbecoming men that strove with Gods.
The lights begin to twinkle from the rocks:
The long day wanes: the slow moon climbs: the deep
Moans round with many voices. Come, my friends,
'Tis not too late to seek a newer world.
Push off, and sitting well in order smite
The sounding furrows; for my purpose holds
To sail beyond the sunset, and the baths
Of all the western stars, until I die.
It may be that the gulfs will wash us down:
It may be we shall touch the Happy Isles,
And see the great Achilles, whom we knew.
Though much is taken, much abides; and though
We are not now that strength which in old days
Moved earth and heaven; that which we are, we are;

One equal temper of heroic hearts,
Made weak by time and fate, but strong in will
To strive, to seek, to find, and not to yield.

Robert Browning (1812–89)

Browning was born in Camberwell, London, and was educated largely at home.
He was 30 before his published poems achieved recognition. A lonely and
intense person, at the age of 34 he secretly married the invalid poet Elizabeth
Barrett and they eloped to Italy to escape her father. Elizabeth Barrett Browning
died fifteen years later, in 1861. Browning divided the remaining years of his life
between England and Italy. His last book of poems was published in London on
the day that he died in Venice at the home of his only son.

This poem is a dramatic monologue; the Duke of Ferrara is negotiating with
an emissary from the father of the woman he hopes to marry.

My last duchess

Ferrara

That's my last Duchess painted on the wall,
Looking as if she were alive. I call
That piece a wonder, now: Frà Pandolf's hands
Worked busily a day, and there she stands.
Will't please you sit and look at her? I said
'Frà Pandolf' by design, for never read
Strangers like you that pictured countenance,
The depth and passion of its earnest glance,
But to myself they turned (since none puts by
The curtain I have drawn for you, but I)
And seemed as they would ask me, if they durst,
How such a glance came there; so, not the first
Are you to turn and ask thus. Sir, 'twas not
Her husband's presence only, called that spot
Of joy into the Duchess' cheek: perhaps
Frà Pandolf chanced to say 'Her mantle laps
Over my lady's wrist too much', or 'Paint
Must never hope to reproduce the faint
Half-flush that dies along her throat': such stuff
Was courtesy, she thought, and cause enough
For calling up that spot of joy. She had
A heart – how shall I say? – too soon made glad,

Too easily impressed; she liked whate'er
She looked on, and her looks went everywhere.
Sir, 'twas all one! My favour at her breast,
The dropping of the daylight in the West,
The bough of cherries some officious fool
Broke in the orchard for her, the white mule
She rode with round the terrace – all and each
Would draw from her alike the approving speech,
Or blush, at least. She thanked men, – good! but thanked ...
Somehow – I know not how – as if she ranked
My gift of a nine-hundred-years-old name
With anybody's gift. Who'd stoop to blame
This sort of trifling? Even had you skill
In speech – (which I have not) – to make your will
Quite clear to such an one, and say, 'Just this
Or that in you disgusts me; here you miss,
Or there exceed the mark' – and if she let
Herself be lessoned so, nor plainly set
Her wits to yours, forsooth, and made excuse,
 – E'en then would be some stooping; and I choose
Never to stoop. Oh sir, she smiled, no doubt,
Whene'er I passed her; but who passed without
Much the same smile? This grew; I gave commands;
Then all smiles stopped together. There she stands
As if alive. Will't please you rise? We'll meet '
The company below, then. I repeat,
The Count your master's known munificence
Is ample warrant that no just pretence
Of mine for dowry will be disallowed;
Though his fair daughter's self, as I avowed
At starting, is my object. Nay, we'll go
Together down, sir. Notice Neptune, though,
Taming a sea-horse, thought a rarity,
Which Claus of Innsbruck cast in bronze for me!

Walt Whitman (1819–92)

Whitman was born on Long Island and had some formal education in Brooklyn, New York. He worked as an office-boy, a printer's assistant, a wandering teacher, and a newspaper editor. After some time in New Orleans he returned to New York and in 1855 published his great work *Leaves of Grass*. Consisting originally of twelve poems (of which 'Song of myself' was the first), it was unorthodox and

strikingly original in its thinking and its form. During the American Civil
War he worked as a volunteer nurse in army hospitals in Washington. He then
became a clerk in the Indian Bureau of the Department of the Interior but was
dismissed because *Leaves of Grass* was considered an 'immoral book'. He lived in
New Jersey for the last twenty years of his life. The extracts that follow give an
idea of the mystical personal experiences that make up the fifty-two 'chants'
of 'Song of myself'.

From Song of myself

1
I celebrate myself,
And what I assume you shall assume,
For every atom belonging to me as good belongs to you.

I loafe and invite my soul,
I lean and loafe at my ease....observing a spear of summer grass.

5
I believe in you my soul....the other I am must not abase itself to you,
And you must not be abased to the other.

Loafe with me on the grass....loose the stop from your throat,
Not words, not music or rhyme I want....not custom or lecture, not
    even the best,
Only the lull I like, the hum of your valved voice.

I mind how we lay in June, such a transparent summer morning;
You settled your head athwart my hips and gently turned over upon me,
And parted the shirt from my bosom-bone, and plunged your tongue to
    my barestript heart,
And reached till you felt my beard, and reached till you held my feet.

Swiftly arose and spread around me the peace and joy and knowledge
    that pass all the art and argument of the earth;
And I know that the hand of God is the elderhand of my own,
And I know that the spirit of God is the eldest brother of my own,
And that all the men ever born are also my brothers....and the women
    my sisters and lovers,
And that a kelson of the creation is love;
And limitless are leaves stiff or drooping in the fields,
And brown ants in the little wells beneath them,
And mossy scabs of the wormfence, and heaped stones, and elder and
    mullen and pokeweed.

17

These are the thoughts of all men in all ages and lands, they are not
     original with me,
If they are not yours as much as mine they are nothing or next to
     nothing,
If they do not enclose everything they are next to nothing,
If they are not the riddle and the untying of the riddle they are nothing,
If they are not as close as they are distant they are nothing.

This is the grass that grows wherever the land is and the water is,
This is the common air that bathes the globe.

This is the breath of laws and songs and behaviour,
This is the tasteless water of souls....this is the true sustenance,
It is for the illiterate....it is for the judges of the supreme court....it is
     for the federal capitol and the state capitols,
It is for the admirable communes of literary men and composers and
     singers and lecturers and engineers and savans,
It is for the endless races of working people and farmers and seamen.

21

I am the poet of the body,
And I am the poet of the soul.

The pleasures of heaven are with me, and the pains of hell are with me,
The first I graft and increase upon myself....the latter I translate into a
     new tongue.

I am the poet of the woman the same as the man,
And I say it is as great to be a woman as to be a man,
And I say there is nothing greater than the mother of men.

* * *

Have you outstript the rest? Are you the President?
It is a trifle....they will more than arrive there every one, and still pass on.

I am he that walks with the tender and growing night;
I call to the earth and sea half-held by the night.

24

Walt Whitman, an American, one of the roughs, a kosmos,
Disorderly fleshy and sensual....eating drinking and breeding,

No sentimentalist....no stander above men and women or apart from
them....no more modest than immodest.

* * *

I dote on myself....there is that lot of me, and all so luscious,
Each moment and whatever happens thrills me with joy.

The dalliance of the eagles

Skirting the river road, (my forenoon walk, my rest,)
Skyward in air a sudden muffled sound, the dalliance of the eagles,
The rushing amorous contact high in space together,
The clinching interlocking claws, a living, fierce, gyrating wheel,
Four beating wings, two beaks, a swirling mass tight grappling,
In tumbling turning clustering loops, straight downward falling,
Till o'er the river poised, the twain yet one, a moment's lull
A motionless still balance in the air, then parting, talons loosing,
Upward again on slow-firm pinions slanting, their separate diverse flight,
She hers, he his, pursuing.

Matthew Arnold (1822–88)

Arnold was the son of Dr Thomas Arnold, the famous headmaster of Rugby
School in Britain, and was educated first at Rugby and then at Oxford. At the age
of 27 he was appointed an Inspector of Schools, a post he held for thirty-seven
years, even while he was Professor of Poetry at Oxford in the 1850s and 1860s.

In 1851, at the age of 29, he married and spent his honeymoon at Dover.
He first published this poem sixteen years later in 1867.

Dover Beach

The sea is calm tonight.
The tide is full, the moon lies fair
Upon the straits; – on the French coast the light
Gleams and is gone; the cliffs of England stand,
Glimmering and vast, out in the tranquil bay.
Come to the window, sweet is the night-air!

Only, from the long line of spray
Where the sea meets the moon-blanched land,
Listen! you hear the grating roar
Of pebbles which the waves draw back, and fling,

At their return, up the high strand,
Begin, and cease, and then again begin,
With tremulous cadence slow, and bring
The eternal note of sadness in.

Sophocles long ago
Heard it on the Aegean, and it brought
Into his mind the turbid ebb and flow
Of human misery; we
Find also in the sound a thought,
Hearing it by this distant northern sea.

The Sea of Faith
Was once, too, at the full, and round earth's shore
Lay like the folds of a bright girdle furled.
But now I only hear
Its melancholy, long, withdrawing roar,
Retreating, to the breath
Of the night-wind, down the vast edges drear
And naked shingles of the world.

Ah, love, let us be true
To one another! for the world, which seems
To lie before us like a land of dreams,
So various, so beautiful, so new,
Hath really neither joy, nor love, nor light,
Nor certitude, nor peace, nor help for pain;
And we are here as on a darkling plain
Swept with confused alarms of struggle and flight,
Where ignorant armies clash by night.

Emily Dickinson (1830–86)

Dickinson lived all of her life in the small town of Amherst in the United States.
She was very reclusive, and preferred to conduct friendships through letter-
writing. Very few of her poems were published during her lifetime, and almost
two thousand were discovered after her death.

Emily Dickinson was rather eccentric in her use of capital letters and
punctuation. One sometimes has to puzzle one's way through this to the
meaning. Early editors used to 'correct' her punctuation and capitalization,
but it is now usual to reprint the poems as she wrote them and not to change
her style.

Because I could not stop for Death

Because I could not stop for Death –
He kindly stopped for me –
The Carriage held but just Ourselves –
And Immortality.

We slowly drove – He knew no haste
And I had put away
My labor and my leisure too,
For His Civility –

We passed the School, where Children strove
At Recess – in the Ring –
We passed the Fields of Gazing Grain –
We passed the Setting Sun –

Or rather – He passed Us –
The Dews drew quivering and chill –
For only Gossamer, my Gown –
My Tippet – only Tulle –

We paused before a House that seemed
A Swelling of the Ground –
The Roof was scarcely visible –
The Cornice – in the Ground – *

Since then – 'tis Centuries – and yet
Feels shorter than the Day
I first surmised the Horses' Heads
Were toward Eternity –

* Another reading of this line is: 'The Cornice – But a Mound –'

Compare this next poem with D H Lawrence's 'Snake' (p. 37).

A narrow Fellow in the Grass

A narrow Fellow in the Grass
Occasionally rides –
You may have met Him – did you not
His notice sudden is –

The Grass divides as with a Comb –
A spotted shaft is seen –
And then it closes at your feet
And opens further on –

He likes a Boggy Acre
A Floor too cool for Corn –
Yet when a Boy, and Barefoot –
I more than once at Noon

Have passed, I thought, a Whip lash
Unbraiding in the Sun
When stooping to secure it
It wrinkled, and was gone –

Several of Nature's People
I know, and they know me –
I feel for them a transport
Of cordiality –

But never met this Fellow
Attended, or alone
Without a tighter breathing
And Zero at the Bone –

They shut me up in Prose

They shut me up in Prose –
As when a little Girl
They put me in the Closet –
Because they liked me 'still'–

Still! Could themself have peeped –
And seen my Brain – go round –
They might as wise have lodged a Bird
For Treason – in the Pound –

Himself has but to will
And easy as a Star
Abolish his Captivity –
And laugh – No more have I –

Gerard Manley Hopkins (1844–89)

Hopkins was born in Stratford, Essex, into a very religious High Anglican
family. While studying classics at Oxford, he converted to Catholicism and
became a Jesuit monk. He always felt a conflict of some kind between, on the
one hand, his enjoyment of natural beauty and his desire to celebrate this in
poetry, and, on the other, his devotion to his religious faith. He was a great
experimenter in sound, stress and rhythm in his poems. Very few of his poems
were published during his lifetime; the first collection appeared twenty-nine
years after his death.

God's grandeur

The world is charged with the grandeur of God.
   It will flame out, like shining from shook foil;
   It gathers to a greatness, like the ooze of oil
Crushed. Why do men then now not reck his rod?
Generations have trod, have trod, have trod;
   And all is seared with trade; bleared, smeared with toil;
   And wears man's smudge and shares man's smell: the soil
Is bare now, nor can foot feel, being shod.

And for all this, nature is never spent;
   There lives the dearest freshness deep down things;
And though the last lights off the black West went
   Oh, morning, at the brown brink eastward, springs –
Because the Holy Ghost over the bent
   World broods with warm breast and with ah! bright wings.

The windhover:

To Christ our Lord

I caught this morning morning's minion, king-
   dom of daylight's dauphin, dapple-dawn-drawn Falcon, in his riding
   Of the rolling level underneath him steady air, and striding
High there, how he rung upon the rein of a wimpling wing
In his ecstasy! then off, off forth on swing,
   As a skate's heel sweeps smooth on a bow-bend: the hurl and gliding
   Rebuffed the big wind. My heart in hiding
Stirred for a bird, – the achieve of, the mastery of the thing!

Brute beauty and valour and act, oh, air, pride, plume, here
   Buckle! AND the fire that breaks from thee then, a billion
Times told lovelier, more dangerous, O my chevalier!

   No wonder of it: shéer plód makes plough down sillion
Shine, and blue-bleak embers, ah my dear,
   Fall, gall themselves, and gash gold-vermilion.

Carrion comfort

Not, I'll not, carrion comfort, Despair, not feast on thee;
Not untwist – slack they may be – these last strands of man
In me ór, most weary, cry *I can no more*. I can;
Can something, hope, wish day come, not choose not to be.
But ah, but O thou terrible, why wouldst thou rude on me
Thy wring-world right foot rock? lay a lionlimb against me? scan
With darksome devouring eyes my bruisèd bones? and fan,
O in turns of tempest, me heaped there; me frantic to avoid thee and flee?

Why? That my chaff might fly; my grain lie, sheer and clear.
Nay in all that toil, that coil, since (seems) I kissed the rod,
Hand rather, my heart lo! lapped strength, stole joy, would laugh, chéer.
Cheer whom though? The hero whose heaven-handling flung me, fóot
   tród
Me? or me that fought him? O which one? is it each one? That night,
   that year
Of now done darkness I wretch lay wrestling with (my God!) my God.

Thou art indeed just, Lord

Thou art indeed just, Lord, if I contend
With thee; but, sir, so what I plead is just.
Why do sinners' ways prosper? and why must
Disappointment all I endeavour end?

   Wert thou my enemy, O thou my friend,
How wouldst thou worse, I wonder, than thou dost
Defeat, thwart me? Oh, the sots and thralls of lust
Do in spare hours more thrive than I that spend,
Sir, life upon thy cause. See, banks and brakes
Now, leavèd how thick! lacèd they are again
With fretty chervil, look, and fresh wind shakes

Them; birds build – but not I build: no, but strain,
Time's eunuch, and not breed one work that wakes.
Mine, O thou lord of life, send my roots rain.

William Butler Yeats (1865–1939)

Yeats was born in Dublin and educated in London and then at the Dublin
School of Art. He was a staunch supporter of the Irish nationalist movement, in
which he worked closely with Lady Gregory; together they founded the Abbey
Theatre, where he became both playwright and director. Coole Park was Lady
Gregory's country estate, which Yeats visited every summer for nineteen years.
Much of the subject matter of Yeats's early poetry was his unrequited love for
Maude Gonne, a beautiful and ardent revolutionary. In 1917 he married Georgie
Hyde-Lees. In 1923 he was awarded the Nobel Prize for Literature.

The wild swans at Coole

The trees are in their autumn beauty,
The woodland paths are dry,
Under the October twilight the water
Mirrors a still sky;
Upon the brimming water among the stones
Are nine-and-fifty swans.

The nineteenth autumn has come upon me
Since I first made my count;
I saw, before I had well finished,
All suddenly mount
And scatter wheeling in great broken rings
Upon their clamorous wings.

I have looked upon those brilliant creatures,
And now my heart is sore.
All's changed since I, hearing at twilight,
The first time on this shore,
The bell-beat of their wings above my head,
Trod with a lighter tread.

Unwearied still, lover by lover,
They paddle in the cold
Companionable streams or climb the air;
Their hearts have not grown old;

Passion or conquest, wander where they will,
Attend upon them still.

But now they drift on the still water,
Mysterious, beautiful;
Among what rushes will they build,
By what lake's edge or pool
Delight men's eyes when I awake some day
To find they have flown away?

How cynical, disillusioned, 'modern', is Yeats's meditation on the great Christian
prophecy and promise? For a different treatment, see Sarah Ruden's poem of the
same name (p. 253). The Nigerian novelist Chinua Achebe made an intriguing
comment when he called his first novel *Things Fall Apart* (see line 3 of the
poem). Achebe's novel traces the breakdown of traditional Nigerian society
as a consequence of the effect of the white Christian missionaries.

The second coming

Turning and turning in the widening gyre
The falcon cannot hear the falconer;
Things fall apart; the centre cannot hold;
Mere anarchy is loosed upon the world,
The blood-dimmed tide is loosed, and everywhere
The ceremony of innocence is drowned;
The best lack all conviction, while the worst
Are full of passionate intensity.

Surely some revelation is at hand;
Surely the Second Coming is at hand.
The Second Coming! Hardly are those words out
When a vast image out of *Spiritus Mundi*
Troubles my sight: somewhere in sands of the desert
A shape with lion body and the head of a man,
A gaze blank and pitiless as the sun,
Is moving its slow thighs, while all about it
Reel shadows of the indignant desert birds.
The darkness drops again; but now I know
That twenty centuries of stony sleep
Were vexed to nightmare by a rocking cradle,
And what rough beast, its hour come round at last,
Slouches towards Bethlehem to be born?

Yeats wrote the following poem when he was 62 and very much concerned about the effects of age, and the decay of the world. 'Byzantium' means Istanbul, here imaged as a kind of earthly eternal paradise. 'That' in line 1 refers to Ireland. 'O sages' in stanza III refers to figures in a Byzantine mosaic he had seen in Ravenna, Sicily. 'Perne' means a spool, here used as a verb, meaning to move with a winding action. 'Gyre' means a spiral. Yeats saw eras of civilization as succeeding series of spirals. Here he perhaps asks the ancient sages to spiral down the cone of time to him.

Sailing to Byzantium

I

That is no country for old men. The young
In one another's arms, birds in the trees
– Those dying generations – at their song,
The salmon-falls, the mackerel-crowded seas,
Fish, flesh, or fowl, commend all summer long
Whatever is begotten, born, and dies.
Caught in that sensual music all neglect
Monuments of unageing intellect.

II

An aged man is but a paltry thing,
A tattered coat upon a stick, unless
Soul clap its hands and sing, and louder sing
For every tatter in its mortal dress,
Nor is there singing school but studying
Monuments of its own magnificence;
And therefore I have sailed the seas and come
To the holy city of Byzantium.

III

O sages standing in God's holy fire
As in the gold mosaic of a wall,
Come from the holy fire, perne in a gyre,
And be the singing-masters of my soul.
Consume my heart away; sick with desire
And fastened to a dying animal
It knows not what it is; and gather me
Into the artifice of eternity.

IV

Once out of nature I shall never take
My bodily form from any natural thing,
But such a form as Grecian goldsmiths make
Of hammered gold and gold enamelling
To keep a drowsy Emperor awake;
Or set upon a golden bough to sing
To lords and ladies of Byzantium
Of what is past, or passing, or to come.

Robert Frost (1874–1963)

Frost was born in the United States of America. He taught as a young man and while staying in England during his thirties, and then settled down in the States. For a time he was an apple farmer in New England. At the age of 87, two years before his death, he became the first poet to be asked to read at a presidential inauguration, that of John F Kennedy. There is a kindly – even folksy – wisdom about much of his poetry (though apparently he could be quite a crusty personality).

Mending wall

Something there is that doesn't love a wall,
That sends the frozen-ground-swell under it
And spills the upper boulders in the sun,
And makes gaps even two can pass abreast.
The work of hunters is another thing:
I have come after them and made repair
Where they have left not one stone on a stone,
But they would have the rabbit out of hiding,
To please the yelping dogs. The gaps I mean,
No one has seen them made or heard them made,
But at spring mending-time we find them there.
I let my neighbor know beyond the hill;
And on a day we meet to walk the line
And set the wall between us once again.
We keep the wall between us as we go.
To each the boulders that have fallen to each.
And some are loaves and some so nearly balls

We have to use a spell to make them balance:
'Stay where you are until our backs are turned!'
We wear our fingers rough with handling them.
Oh, just another kind of outdoor game,
One on a side. It comes to little more:
There where it is we do not need the wall:
He is all pine and I am apple orchard.
My apple trees will never get across
And eat the cones under his pines, I tell him.
He only says, 'Good fences make good neighbors.'
Spring is the mischief in me, and I wonder
If I could put a notion in his head:
'*Why* do they make good neighbors? Isn't it
Where there are cows? But here there are no cows.
Before I built a wall I'd ask to know
What I was walling in or walling out,
And to whom I was like to give offense.
Something there is that doesn't love a wall,
That wants it down.' I could say 'Elves' to him,
But it's not elves exactly, and I'd rather
He said it for himself. I see him there,
Bringing a stone grasped firmly by the top
In each hand, like an old-stone savage armed.
He moves in darkness as it seems to me,
Not of woods only and the shade of trees.
He will not go behind his father's saying.
And he likes having thought of it so well
He says again, 'Good fences make good neighbors.'

Stopping by woods on a snowy evening

Whose woods these are I think I know.
His house is in the village, though;
He will not see me stopping here
To watch his woods fill up with snow.

My little horse must think it queer
To stop without a farmhouse near
Between the woods and frozen lake
The darkest evening of the year.

He gives his harness bells a shake
To ask if there is some mistake.
The only other sound's the sweep
Of easy wind and downy flake.

The woods are lovely, dark and deep,
But I have promises to keep,
And miles to go before I sleep,
And miles to go before I sleep.

The title of the next poem is drawn from Shakespeare's play *Macbeth*. In thinking of how precarious our hold is on life, Macbeth says, 'Out, out, brief candle.'

'Out, out –'

The buzz saw snarled and rattled in the yard
And made dust and dropped stove-length sticks of wood,
Sweet-scented stuff when the breeze drew across it.
And from there those that lifted eyes could count
Five mountain ranges one behind the other
Under the sunset far into Vermont.
And the saw snarled and rattled, snarled and rattled,
As it ran light, or had to bear a load.
And nothing happened: day was all but done.
Call it a day, I wish they might have said
To please the boy by giving him the half hour
That a boy counts so much when saved from work.
His sister stood beside them in her apron
To tell them 'Supper.' At the word, the saw,
As if to prove saws knew what supper meant,
Leaped out at the boy's hand, or seemed to leap –
He must have given the hand. However it was,
Neither refused the meeting. But the hand!
The boy's first outcry was a rueful laugh,
As he swung toward them holding up the hand,
Half in appeal, but half as if to keep
The life from spilling. Then the boy saw all –
Since he was old enough to know, big boy
Doing a man's work, though a child at heart –

He saw all spoiled. 'Don't let him cut my hand off –
The doctor, when he comes. Don't let him, sister!'
So. But the hand was gone already.
The doctor put him in the dark of ether.
He lay and puffed his lips out with his breath.
And then – the watcher at his pulse took fright.
No one believed. They listened at his heart.
Little – less – nothing! – and that ended it.
No more to build on there. And they, since they
Were not the one dead, turned to their affairs.

William Carlos Williams (1883–1963)

Williams was born in the small country town of Rutherford in New Jersey in
the United States. He studied medicine at the University of Pennsylvania. In 1910
he settled as a doctor, back in Rutherford. Two years later he married his wife
Flossie. He continued to live and practise in Rutherford, together with his wife,
right through to his death in 1963 at the age of 80. Over the years he published
more than seventeen volumes of poems, and was the adviser and friend of nearly
all the important poets in America.

Compare the attitude to fading beauty in this next poem to that in the
poems of Christopher Marlowe (p. 3), Sir Walter Ralegh (p. 4) and William
Shakespeare (p. 5).

The act

There were the roses, in the rain.
Don't cut them, I pleaded.
          They won't last, she said.
But they're so beautiful
          where they are.
Agh, we were all beautiful once, she
          said,
and cut them and gave them to me
          in my hand.

The artist

Mr. T.
          bareheaded
                    in a soiled undershirt

his hair standing out
        on all sides
                stood on his toes
heels together
        arms gracefully
                for the moment
curled above his head.
        Then he whirled about
                bounded
into the air
        and with an *entrechat*
                perfectly achieved
completed the figure.
        My mother
                taken by surprise
where she sat
        in her invalid's chair
                was left speechless.
Bravo! she cried at last
        and clapped her hands.
                The man's wife
came from the kitchen:
        What goes on here? she said.
                But the show was over.

Dr Williams left Flossie this note after returning home from a late-night call.

This is just to say

I have eaten
the plums
that were in
the icebox

and which
you were probably
saving
for breakfast

Forgive me
they were delicious
so sweet
and so cold

D H (David Herbert) Lawrence (1885–1930)

Lawrence was born in a coal-mining village in Nottinghamshire in England, the son of a miner father and a schoolteacher mother. He eloped with Frieda Weekley, the German wife of his university tutor. They travelled around the world a great deal: Sicily, Australia, Mexico, Italy. He died of tuberculosis in Vence in the South of France. His body was later disinterred, cremated, and the ashes placed in a shrine on his Lobo Mountain ranch in Taos in New Mexico in the United States.

Snake

A snake came to my water-trough
On a hot, hot day, and I in pyjamas for the heat,
To drink there.

In the deep, strange-scented shade of the great dark carob-tree
I came down the steps with my pitcher
And must wait, must stand and wait, for there he was at the trough
    before me.

He reached down from a fissure in the earth-wall in the gloom
And trailed his yellow-brown slackness soft-bellied down, over the edge
    of the stone trough
And rested his throat upon the stone bottom,
And where the water had dripped from the tap, in a small clearness,
He sipped with his straight mouth,
Softly drank through his straight gums, into his slack long body,
Silently.

Someone was before me at my water-trough,
And I, like a second comer, waiting.

He lifted his head from his drinking, as cattle do,
And looked at me vaguely, as drinking cattle do,
And flickered his two-forked tongue from his lips, and mused a moment,
And stooped and drank a little more,
Being earth-brown, earth-golden from the burning bowels of the earth
On the day of Sicilian July, with Etna smoking.

The voice of my education said to me
He must be killed,
For in Sicily the black, black snakes are innocent, the gold are venomous.

And voices in me said, If you were a man
You would take a stick and break him now, and finish him off.

But must I confess how I liked him,
How glad I was he had come like a guest in quiet, to drink at my water-
      trough
And depart peaceful, pacified, and thankless,
Into the burning bowels of this earth.

Was it cowardice, that I dared not kill him?
Was it perversity, that I longed to talk to him?
Was it humility, to feel so honoured?
I felt so honoured.

And yet those voices:
If you were not afraid, you would kill him!

And truly I was afraid, I was most afraid,
But even so, honoured still more
That he should seek my hospitality
From out the dark door of the secret earth.

He drank enough
And lifted his head, dreamily, as one who has drunken,
And flickered his tongue like a forked night on the air, so black,
Seeming to lick his lips,
And looked around like a god, unseeing, into the air,
And slowly turned his head,
And slowly, very slowly, as if thrice adream,
Proceeded to draw his slow length curving round
And climb again the broken bank of my wall-face.

And as he put his head into that dreadful hole,
And as he slowly drew up, snake-easing his shoulders, and entered farther,
A sort of horror, a sort of protest against his withdrawing into that
      horrid black hole,
Deliberately going into the blackness, and slowly drawing himself after,
Overcame me now his back was turned.

I looked around, I put down my pitcher,
I picked up a clumsy log
And threw it at the water-trough with a clatter.

I think it did not hit him,
But suddenly that part of him that was left behind convulsed in
     undignified haste,
Writhed like lightning, and was gone
Into the black hole, the earth-lipped fissure in the wall-front,
At which, in the intense still noon, I stared with fascination.

And immediately I regretted it.
I thought how paltry, how vulgar, what a mean act!
I despised myself and the voices of my accursed human education.
And I thought of the albatross,
And I wished he would come back, my snake.

For he seemed to me again like a king,
Like a king in exile, uncrowned in the underworld,
Now due to be crowned again.

And so, I missed my chance with one of the lords
Of life.
And I have something to expiate;
A pettiness.

Rupert Brooke (1887–1915)

Brooke was educated at Rugby and at Cambridge. After a serious breakdown he
travelled to Tahiti in the Pacific. On the outbreak of war in 1914 he enlisted, took
part in the Antwerp expedition, and then died of blood-poisoning on the way to
the Dardanelles.

   This poem was written right at the start of the war, and gives the idealized
view of the war initially held by young men. It needs to be read beside Wilfred
Owen's war poems, which were written later in the war, in 1917 and 1918 (p. 46).

Peace

Now, God be thanked Who has matched us with His hour,
     And caught our youth, and wakened us from sleeping,
With hand made sure, clear eye, and sharpened power,
     To turn, as swimmers into cleanness leaping,
Glad from a world grown old and cold and weary,
     Leave the sick hearts that honour could not move,
And half-men, and their dirty songs and dreary,
     And all the little emptiness of love!

Oh! we, who have known shame, we have found release there,
  Where there's no ill, no grief, but sleep has mending.
    Naught broken save this body, lost but breath;
  Nothing to shake the laughing heart's long peace there
    But only agony, and that has ending;
      And the worst friend and enemy is but Death.

T S (Thomas Stearns) Eliot (1888–1965)

Eliot was born in St Louis, Missouri, in the United States. He studied at Harvard University, the Sorbonne in Paris, and then in 1914 moved to England to study at Oxford. He remained in the United Kingdom. He worked first as a banker and then as a publisher. He became the most highly respected poet and critic of his time, and was awarded the Nobel Prize for Literature at the age of 60.

'Preludes' is a young man's poem, written in 1910–11 while he was a student, and he has in mind Roxbury, a rundown area of Boston.

Preludes

I

The winter evening settles down
With smell of steaks in passageways.
Six o'clock.
The burnt-out ends of smoky days.
And now a gusty shower wraps
The grimy scraps
Of withered leaves about your feet
And newspapers from vacant lots;
The showers beat
On broken blinds and chimney-pots,
And at the corner of the street
A lonely cab-horse steams and stamps.

And then the lighting of the lamps.

II

The morning comes to consciousness
Of faint stale smells of beer
From the sawdust-trampled street

With all its muddy feet that press
To early coffee-stands.

With the other masquerades
That time resumes,
One thinks of all the hands
That are raising dingy shades
In a thousand furnished rooms.

III

You tossed a blanket from the bed,
You lay upon your back, and waited;
You dozed, and watched the night revealing
The thousand sordid images
Of which your soul was constituted;
They flickered against the ceiling.
And when all the world came back
And the light crept up between the shutters
And you heard the sparrows in the gutters,
You had such a vision of the street
As the street hardly understands;
Sitting along the bed's edge, where
You curled the papers from your hair,
Or clasped the yellow soles of feet
In the palms of both soiled hands.

IV

His soul stretched tight across the skies
That fade behind a city block,
Or trampled by insistent feet
At four and five and six o'clock;
And short square fingers stuffing pipes,
And evening newspapers, and eyes
Assured of certain certainties,
The conscience of a blackened street
Impatient to assume the world.

I am moved by fancies that are curled
Around these images, and cling:
The notion of some infinitely gentle
Infinitely suffering thing.

....

Wipe your hand across your mouth, and laugh;
The worlds revolve like ancient women
Gathering fuel in vacant lots.

The next poem was written after Eliot's conversion to Anglo-Catholicism.
A 'Magus' is a wise man. The first five lines are in inverted commas because they
are quoted from a seventeenth-century sermon given by the then Archbishop of
Canterbury. Nigerian novelist Chinua Achebe's second novel is called *No Longer
at Ease*, an allusion to this poem (see the third-last line). The novel deals with
the differences in the traditionalist and colonialist orders in Nigeria. In the
poem, watch out for a number of forward-looking references to events
connected with Jesus's life and death.

Journey of the Magi

'A cold coming we had of it,
Just the worst time of the year
For a journey, and such a long journey:
The ways deep and the weather sharp,
The very dead of winter.'
And the camels galled, sore-footed, refractory,
Lying down in the melting snow.
There were times we regretted
The summer palaces on slopes, the terraces,
And the silken girls bringing sherbet.
Then the camel men cursing and grumbling
And running away, and wanting their liquor and women,
And the night-fires going out, and the lack of shelters,
And the cities hostile, and the towns unfriendly
And the villages dirty and charging high prices:
A hard time we had of it.
At the end we preferred to travel all night,
Sleeping in snatches,
With the voices singing in our ears, saying
That this was all folly.

Then at dawn we came down to a temperate valley,
Wet, below the snow line, smelling of vegetation;
With a running stream and a water-mill beating the darkness,
And three trees on the low sky.
And an old white horse galloped away in the meadow.

Then we came to a tavern with vine-leaves over the lintel,
Six hands at an open door dicing for pieces of silver,
And feet kicking the empty wine-skins.
But there was no information, and so we continued
And arrived at evening, not a moment too soon
Finding the place; it was (you may say) satisfactory.

    All this was a long time ago, I remember,
And I would do it again, but set down
This set down
This: were we led all that way for
Birth or Death? There was a Birth, certainly,
We had evidence and no doubt. I had seen birth and death,
But had thought they were different; this Birth was
Hard and bitter agony for us, like Death, our death.
We returned to our places, these Kingdoms,
But no longer at ease here, in the old dispensation,
With an alien people clutching their gods.
I should be glad of another death.

The next poem, written in 1921–22 while Eliot was also working on his major
poem 'The Waste Land', is rich in associations. Three of its main associations
are the Gunpowder Plot of 5 November 1605, Shakespeare's *Julius Caesar* and
Joseph Conrad's novella *The Heart of Darkness*. The title and the two epigraphs
at the start of the poem combine all three: the straw-stuffed effigy of Guy Fawkes
that children use to collect money for fireworks; in Shakespeare's play, Brutus
refers to the conspirators as 'hollow men'; and in Conrad's novella, Mr Kurtz
is described as a 'hollow sham' and 'hollow at the core'. A fourth source of
reference throughout the poem is Dante's poem *Divina Commedia*, with 'death's
dream kingdom' ('Inferno', or hell), 'death's other kingdom' ('Paradiso', or
heaven), and 'death's twilight kingdom' (the earthly paradise where Dante
meets his loved one Beatrice).

The hollow men

Mistah Kurtz – he dead

A penny for the Old Guy

I

We are the hollow men
We are the stuffed men
Leaning together

Headpiece filled with straw. Alas!
Our dried voices, when
We whisper together
Are quiet and meaningless
As wind in dry grass
Or rats' feet over broken glass
In our dry cellar

Shape without form, shade without colour,
Paralysed force, gesture without motion;

Those who have crossed
With direct eyes, to death's other Kingdom
Remember us – if at all – not as lost
Violent souls, but only
As the hollow men
The stuffed men.

II

Eyes I dare not meet in dreams
In death's dream kingdom
These do not appear:
There, the eyes are
Sunlight on a broken column
There, is a tree swinging
And voices are
In the wind's singing
More distant and more solemn
Than a fading star.

Let me be no nearer
In death's dream kingdom
Let me also wear
Such deliberate disguises
Rat's coat, crowskin, crossed staves
In a field
Behaving as the wind behaves
No nearer –

Not that final meeting
In the twilight kingdom

III

This is the dead land
This is cactus land
Here the stone images
Are raised, here they receive
The supplication of a dead man's hand
Under the twinkle of a fading star.

Is it like this
In death's other kingdom
Waking alone
At the hour when we are
Trembling with tenderness
Lips that would kiss
Form prayers to broken stone.

IV

The eyes are not here
There are no eyes here
In this valley of dying stars
In this hollow valley
This broken jaw of our lost kingdoms

In this last of meeting places
We grope together
And avoid speech
Gathered on this beach of the tumid river

Sightless, unless
The eyes reappear
As the perpetual star
Multifoliate rose
Of death's twilight kingdom
The hope only
Of empty men.

V

Here we go round the prickly pear
Prickly pear prickly pear
Here we go round the prickly pear
At five o'clock in the morning.

Between the idea
And the reality
Between the motion
And the act
Falls the Shadow

For Thine is the Kingdom

Between the conception
And the creation
Between the emotion
And the response
Falls the Shadow

Life is very long

Between the desire
And the spasm
Between the potency
And the existence
Between the essence
And the descent
Falls the Shadow

For Thine is the Kingdom

For Thine is
Life is
For Thine is the

This is the way the world ends
This is the way the world ends
This is the way the world ends
Not with a bang but a whimper.

Wilfred Owen (1893–1918)

Owen was born in the United Kingdom. Like Keats, Owen was only 25 when he died on 4 November 1918, one week before the First World War ended; the telegram informing his parents of his death was delivered to them as the armistice bells were ringing on 11 November 1918. A young officer in the trench warfare of 1917–18, Owen was leading his men across a canal when he was shot dead. He had suffered a severe nervous breakdown during his time at the front as a result of his experiences. No poet has ever given so vivid an account of what it means to be in the middle of a war. Before you read the Owen poems that follow, read Rupert Brooke's poem 'Peace' on p. 39 to see the idealized, romantic notion of war that the young men of Britain held a few years before, at the start of the war in 1914.

'Passing-bells' are church bells rung for the dead. Blinds were drawn down in a house where there had been a death. This sonnet sets the conventional church ritualization of death against the crude experience of death in the heat of battle, itself a kind of ritual.

Anthem for doomed youth

What passing-bells for these who die as cattle?
    Only the monstrous anger of the guns.
    Only the stuttering rifles' rapid rattle
Can patter out their hasty orisons.
No mockeries now for them; no prayers nor bells,
    Nor any voice of mourning save the choirs, –
The shrill, demented choirs of wailing shells;
    And bugles calling for them from sad shires.

What candles may be held to speed them all?
    Not in the hands of boys, but in their eyes
Shall shine the holy glimmers of good-byes.
    The pallor of girls' brows shall be their pall;
Their flowers the tenderness of patient minds,
And each slow dusk a drawing-down of blinds.

'Boche' is a British wartime slang-word for 'German'. Owen described this incident involving a blinded sentry in a letter to his mother a year and eight months before he wrote this poem.

The sentry

We'd found an old Boche dug-out, and he knew,
And gave us hell, for shell on frantic shell
Hammered on top, but never quite burst through.
Rain, guttering down in waterfalls of slime
Kept slush waist-high and rising hour by hour,
And choked the steps too thick with clay to climb.
What murk of air remained stank old, and sour

With fumes of whizz-bangs, and the smell of men
Who'd lived there years, and left their curse in the den,
If not their corpses...
                    There we herded from the blast
Of whizz-bangs, but one found our door at last, –
Buffeting eyes and breath, snuffing the candles.
And thud! flump! thud! down the steep steps came thumping
And sploshing in the flood, deluging muck –
The sentry's body; then, his rifle, handles
Of old Boche bombs, and mud in ruck on ruck.
We dredged him up, for killed, until he whined
'O sir, my eyes – I'm blind – I'm blind, I'm blind!'
Coaxing, I held a flame against his lids
And said if he could see the least blurred light
He was not blind; in time he'd get all right.
'I can't,' he sobbed. Eyeballs, huge-bulged like squids',
Watch my dreams still; but I forgot him there
In posting Next for duty, and sending a scout
To beg a stretcher somewhere, and flound'ring about
To other posts under the shrieking air.

                    * * *

Those other wretches, how they bled and spewed,
And one who would have drowned himself for good, –
I try not to remember these things now.
Let dread hark back for one word only: how
Half listening to that sentry's moans and jumps,
And the wild chattering of his broken teeth,
Renewed most horribly whenever crumps
Pummelled the roof and slogged the air beneath –
Through the dense din, I say, we heard him shout
'I see your lights!' But ours had long died out.

Perhaps the next poem was not entirely completed before Owen's death.
Apart from the strange blurring of dream and real experience, look carefully
at the way Owen has mastered the use of half-rhyme or part-rhyme to create
an uneasy, discordant atmosphere (for example 'escaped'/'scooped' and
'groined'/'groaned': they just miss the rhyme, and so we are left feeling
uncomfortable).

Strange meeting

It seemed that out of battle I escaped
Down some profound dull tunnel, long since scooped
Through granites which titanic wars had groined.
Yet also there encumbered sleepers groaned,
Too fast in thought or death to be bestirred.
Then, as I probed them, one sprang up, and stared
With piteous recognition in fixed eyes,
Lifting distressful hands as if to bless.
And by his smile, I knew that sullen hall,
By his dead smile I knew we stood in Hell.
With a thousand pains that vision's face was grained;
Yet no blood reached there from the upper ground,
And no guns thumped, or down the flues made moan.
'Strange friend,' I said, 'here is no cause to mourn.'
'None,' said that other, 'save the undone years,
The hopelessness. Whatever hope is yours,
Was my life also; I went hunting wild
After the wildest beauty in the world,
Which lies not calm in eyes, or braided hair,
But mocks the steady running of the hour,
And if it grieves, grieves richlier than here.
For by my glee might many men have laughed,
And of my weeping something had been left,
Which must die now. I mean the truth untold,
The pity of war, the pity war distilled.
Now men will go content with what we spoiled,
Or, discontent, boil bloody, and be spilled.
They will be swift with swiftness of the tigress.
None will break ranks, though nations trek from progress.
Courage was mine, and I had mystery,
Wisdom was mine, and I had mastery:
To miss the march of this retreating world
Into vain citadels that are not walled.
Then, when much blood had clogged their chariot-wheels,
I would go up and wash them from sweet wells,
Even with truths that lie too deep for taint.
I would have poured my spirit without stint
But not through wounds; not on the cess of war.
Foreheads of men have bled where no wounds were.
I am the enemy you killed, my friend.

I knew you in this dark; for so you frowned
Yesterday through me as you jabbed and killed.
I parried; but my hands were loath and cold.
Let us sleep now …'

e e (Edward Estlin) cummings (1894–1962)

Cummings was born in Cambridge, Massachusetts, in the United States, and graduated from Harvard University. In 1917 he served with an ambulance unit in France and, mistakenly suspected of espionage, was interned in a French detention camp. Throughout his life he was both a painter and a poet. He experimented with using words in unusual ways. Similarly, he was unorthodox in his use of punctuation and typography.

i thank You God for most this amazing

i thank You God for most this amazing
day:for the leaping greenly spirits of trees
and a blue true dream of sky;and for everything
which is natural which is infinite which is yes

(i who have died am alive again today,
and this is the sun's birthday;this is the birth
day of life and of love and wings:and of the gay
great happening illimitably earth)

how should tasting touching hearing seeing
breathing any—lifted from the no
of all nothing—human merely being
doubt unimaginable You?

(now the ears of my ears awake and
now the eyes of my eyes are opened)

in Just-

in Just-
spring   when the world is mud-
luscious the little
lame balloonman

whistles   far   and wee

and eddieandbill come
running from marbles and
piracies and it's
spring

when the world is puddle-wonderful

the queer
old balloonman whistles
far   and   wee
and bettyandisbel come dancing

from hop-scotch and jump-rope and

it's
spring
and
    the

       goat-footed

balloonMan   whistles
far
and
wee

my sweet old etcetera

my sweet old etcetera
aunt lucy during the recent

war could and what
is more did tell you just
what everybody was fighting

for,
my sister

isabel created hundreds
(and
hundreds)of socks not to
mention shirts fleaproof earwarmers

etcetera wristers etcetera, my
mother hoped that

i would die etcetera
bravely of course my father used
to become hoarse talking about how it was
a privilege and if only he
could meanwhile my

self etcetera lay quietly
in the deep mud et

cetera
(dreaming,
et

   cetera,of
Your smile
eyes knees and of your Etcetera)

Roy Campbell (1901–57)

Campbell was born and educated in Durban, spent a year at Oxford, and then, after a short return to Durban, lived in various Mediterranean countries. He was mercurial and contradictory in both his politics and his personality. In the 1930s he supported Franco in Spain, Mussolini in Italy, and Hitler in Germany; in the 1940s he enlisted in the British army to fight them. He died in a car crash in Portugal.

On some South African novelists

You praise the firm restraint with which they write –
I'm with you there, of course:
They use the snaffle and the curb all right,
But where's the bloody horse?

On the same

Far from the vulgar haunts of men
Each sits in her 'successful room',
Housekeeping with her fountain pen
And writing novels with her broom.

Langston Hughes (1902–67)

For over forty years Hughes was the poetic voice of African Americans. His father had abandoned the United States and gone to live in Mexico. After finishing school, Langston Hughes spent a year living with his father, but then returned to the States. He spent a year studying at Columbia University, then joined the merchant navy, and spent some time in Paris. He became one of the leaders of the 'Black Renaissance' in Harlem, New York. The first of many collections of poems *The Weary Blues* was published in 1926.

Compare this next poem with Anne Sexton's 'Wanting to die' (p. 117).

Life is fine

I went down to the river,
I set down on the bank.
I tried to think but couldn't,
So I jumped in and sank.

I came up once and hollered!
I came up twice and cried!
If that water hadn't a-been so cold
I might've sunk and died.

But it was
Cold in that water!
It was cold!

I took the elevator
Sixteen floors above the ground.
I thought about my baby
And thought I would jump down.

I stood there and I hollered!
I stood there and I cried!
If it hadn't a-been so high
I might've jumped and died.

But it was
High up there!
It was high!

So since I'm still here livin',
I guess I will live on.
I could've died for love –
But for livin' I was born.

Though you may hear me holler,
And you may see me cry –
I'll be dogged, sweet baby,
If you gonna see me die.

> *Life is fine!*
> *Fine as wine!*
> *Life is fine!*

Madam and the rent man

The rent man knocked.
He said, Howdy-do?
I said, What
Can I do for you?
He said, You know
Your rent is due.

I said, Listen,
Before I'd pay
I'd go to Hades
And rot away!

The sink is broke,
The water don't run,
And you ain't done a thing
You promised to've done.

Back window's cracked,
Kitchen floor squeaks,
There's rats in the cellar,
And the attic leaks.

He said, Madam,
It's not up to me.
I'm just the agent,
Don't you see?

I said, Naturally,
You pass the buck.
If it's money you want,
You're out of luck.

He said, Madam,
I ain't pleased!
I said, Neither am I.

So we agrees!

Stevie Smith (1902–71)

Smith was brought up in Palmers Green, north London, where she spent most of her adult life. Her poems have been described as 'witty, caustic, and enigmatic [puzzling]'.

Away, melancholy

Away, melancholy,
Away with it, let it go.

Are not the trees green,
The earth as green?
Does not the wind blow,
Fire leap and the rivers flow?
Away, melancholy.

The ant is busy
He carrieth his meat,
All things hurry
To be eaten or eat.
Away, melancholy.

Man, too, hurries,
Eats, couples, buries,
He is an animal also
With a hey ho melancholy,
Away with it, let it go.

Man of all creatures
Is superlative
(Away melancholy)
He of all creatures alone
Raiseth a stone
(Away melancholy)

Into the stone, the god,
Pours what he knows of good
Calling good, God.
Away, melancholy, let it go.

Speak not to me of tears,
Tyranny, pox, wars,
Saying, Can God,
Stone of man's thought, be good?

Say rather it is enough
That the stuffed
Stone of man's good, growing,
By man's called God.
Away, melancholy, let it go.

Man aspires
To good,
To love
Sighs;

Beaten, corrupted, dying
In his own blood lying
Yet heaves up an eye above
Cries, Love, love.
It is his virtue needs explaining,
Not his failing.

Away, melancholy,
Away with it, let it go.

Not waving but drowning

Nobody heard him, the dead man,
But still he lay moaning:
I was much further out than you thought
And not waving but drowning.

Poor chap, he always loved larking
And now he's dead
It must have been too cold for him his heart gave way,
They said.

Oh, no no no, it was too cold always
(Still the dead one lay moaning)
I was much too far out all my life
And not waving but drowning.

Alan Paton (1903 – 88)

Paton was born in Pietermaritzburg. After qualifying at the Natal University
College, he taught for some years, and then became the principal of the
Diepkloof Reformatory, a post he held for thirteen years. His educational
reforms there were highly respected. In 1948 he wrote the best-selling novel that
was to make him internationally known, *Cry the Beloved Country*. He later
became the president of the Liberal Party. In 1960 his passport was confiscated.

Compare this poem with Mavis Smallberg's 'A small boy' (p. 217), written
thirty-seven years after Paton's 1949 poem.

To a small boy who died at Diepkloof Reformatory

Small offender, small innocent child
With no conception or comprehension
Of the vast machinery set in motion
By your trivial transgression,
Of the great forces of authority,
Of judges, magistrates, and lawyers,
Psychologists, psychiatrists, and doctors,
Principals, police, and sociologists,
Kept moving and alive by your delinquency,
This day, and under the shining sun
Do I commit your body to the earth
Oh child, oh lost and lonely one.

Clerks are moved to action by your dying;
Your documents, all neatly put together,
Are transferred from the living to the dead,
Here is the document of birth
Saying that you were born and where and when,
But giving no hint of joy or sorrow,
Or if the sun shone, or if the rain was falling,
Or what bird flew singing over the roof
Where your mother travailed. And here your name
Meaning in white man's tongue, he is arrived,
But to what end or purpose is not said.

Here is the last certificate of Death;
Forestalling authority he sets you free,
You that did once arrive have now departed
And are enfolded in the sole embrace
Of kindness that earth ever gave to you.
So negligent in life, in death belatedly
She pours her generous abundance on you
And rains her bounty on the quivering wood
And swaddles you about, where neither hail nor tempest,
Neither wind nor snow nor any heat of sun
Shall now offend you, and the thin cold spears
Of the highveld rain that once so pierced you
In falling on your grave shall press you closer
To the deep repentant heart.

Here is the warrant of committal,
For this offence, oh small and lonely one,
For this offence in whose commission
Millions of men are in complicity
You are committed. So do I commit you,
Your frail body to the waiting ground,
Your dust to the dust of the veld, –
Fly home-bound soul to the great Judge-President
Who unencumbered by the pressing need
To give society protection, may pass on you
The sentence of the indeterminate compassion.

William Plomer (1903–73)

Plomer was born in Pietersburg in what is now the Northern Province. After going to school in South Africa and at Rugby in the United Kingdom, he farmed in the Stormberg and was a trader in KwaZulu-Natal. He left South Africa in 1926, going first to Japan and then to the United Kingdom.

The author provided this note to the next poem: 'In memory of the poet Ingrid Jonker, who was found dead by night at Sea Point, Cape Town, in July, 1965; and of Nathaniel Nakasa, the South African writer, who died by suicide in the United States in the same month.'

Ingrid Jonker was a young Afrikaans poet, daughter of a leading member of the National Party, who felt entirely estranged from her father, his family and their culture. At the time of her suicide by drowning, aged 32, she had a young daughter, and had recently returned from an unhappy trip to Europe. The writer Jack Cope, twenty years older than Jonker, was the friend referred to in the fourth stanza. Nat Nakasa was an energetic young writer who took up a scholarship in the United States even though the South African government had refused him a passport and offered him only a one-way exit permit. He threw himself out of a building in New York. He was 28 when he died.

The taste of the fruit

Where a dry tide of sheep
Ebbs between rocks
In a miasma of dust,
Where time is wool;
He is not there.

Where towers of green water
Crash, re-shaping
White contours of sand,
Velvet to a bare foot;
She is not there.

Where pride in modesty,
Grace, neatness,
Glorify the slum shack
Of one pensive woman;
He is not there.

Where one fatherly man
Waited with absolute
Understanding, undemanding
Hands full of comfort;
She is not there.

Where sour beer and thick smoke,
Lewdness and loud
Laughter half disguise
Hope dying of wounds;
He is not there.

Where meat-fed men are idling
On a deep stoep,
Voicing disapproval
Of those who have 'views';
She is not there.

Where with hands tied
They wrestle for freedom;
Where with mouth stopped
They ripen a loud cry;
He is not there.

Where intellectuals
Bunch together to follow
Fashions that allow for
No private exceptions;
She is not there.

He, who loved learning,
Nimbly stood up to
The heavyweight truth;
For long years in training
He is not there.

She was thought childlike
But carried the iron
Seeds of knowledge and wisdom;
Where they now flower,
She is not there.

A man with no passport,
He had leave to exile
Himself from the natural
Soil of his being,
But none to return.

She, with a passport,
Turned great eyes on Europe.
What did she return to?
She found, back home, that
She was not there.

Now he is free in
A state with no frontiers,
But where men are working
To undermine frontiers,
He is not there.

'My people,' in anguish
She cried, 'from me have rotted

Utterly away.' Everywhere
She felt rejected;
Now she is nowhere.

Where men waste in prison
For trying to be fruitful,
The first fruit is setting
Themselves fought for;
He will not taste it.

Her blood and his
Fed the slow, tormented
Tree that is destined
To bear what will be
Bough-bending plenty.

Let those who savour
Ripeness and sweetness,
Let them taste and remember
Him, her, and all others
Secreted in the juices.

C (Cecil) Day Lewis (1904–72)

Day Lewis was born in Ireland and educated at Oxford, where he became
friendly with the young poets led by W H Auden. In 1936 he joined the
Communist Party and supported socialism. He was later to become
disillusioned, and became an increasingly establishment figure. Under the
pseudonym Nicholas Blake he wrote many detective novels. He was Professor
of Poetry at Oxford from 1951 to 1956. He became Poet Laureate in 1968, which
means that he was required to write poems on state occasions. He had two sons:
Sean, to whom this poem is dedicated and who later wrote a book about his
father, and the actor, Daniel Day Lewis.

Walking away

for Sean

It is eighteen years ago, almost to the day –
A sunny day with the leaves just turning,
The touch-lines new-ruled – since I watched you play
Your first game of football, then, like a satellite
Wrenched from its orbit, go drifting away

Behind a scatter of boys. I can see
You walking away from me towards the school
With the pathos of a half-fledged thing set free
Into a wilderness, the gait of one
Who finds no path where the path should be.

That hesitant figure, eddying away
Like a winged seed loosened from its parent stem,
Has something I never quite grasp to convey
About nature's give-and-take – the small, the scorching
Ordeals which fire one's irresolute clay.

I have had worse partings, but none that so
Gnaws at my mind still. Perhaps it is roughly
Saying what God alone could perfectly show –
How selfhood begins with a walking away,
And love is proved in the letting go.

Read this poem as a modern 1930s' response to or comment on Christopher
Marlowe's and Walter Ralegh's poems (pp. 3 and 4).

Come, live with me and be my love

Come, live with me and be my love,
And we will all the pleasures prove
Of peace and plenty, bed and board,
That chance employment may afford.

I'll handle dainties on the docks
And thou shalt read of summer frocks:
At evening by the sour canals
We'll hope to hear some madrigals.

Care on thy maiden brow shall put
A wreath of wrinkles, and thy foot
Be shod with pain: not silken dress
But toil shall tire thy loveliness.

Hunger shall make thy modest zone
And cheat fond death of all but bone –
If these delights thy mind may move,
Then live with me and be my love.

Earle Birney (1904–95)

Birney was born in Calgary in Alberta, Canada. He was educated at the Universities of British Columbia and Toronto and has taught at American and Canadian universities.

This poem was written about a visit to Trinidad.

Meeting of strangers

'Nice jacket you gat deh, man!'

He swerved his bicycle toward my curb
to call   then flashed around the corner
a blur in the dusk   of somebody big
redshirted   young   dark   unsmiling

As I stood waiting for a taxi to show
I thought him droll at least
A passing pleasantry? It was frayed
a sixdollar coat   tropical weight
in this heat only something with pockets
to carry things in

Now all four streets were empty
Dockland   everything shut
It was a sound no bigger than a breath
that made me wheel

He was ten feet away   redshirt
The cycle leant by a post farther off
where an alley came in   What?!

My turning froze him
in the middle of some elaborate stealth
He looked almost comic   splayed
but there was a glitter
under the downheld hand
and something smoked from his eyes

By God if I was going to be stabbed
for my wallet (adrenalin suffused me)
it would have to be done in plain sight
I made a flying leap
to the middle of the crossing

White man tourist surrogate yes
but not guilty enough
to be skewered in the guts for it
without raising all Trinidad first
with shouts fists feet whatever
– I squared round to meet him

and there was a beautiful taxi
lumbering in from a sidestreet
empty!

As I rolled away   safe as Elijah
lucky as Ganymede
there on the curb I'd leaped from
stood that damned cyclist solemnly
shouting

'What did he say?' I asked the driver
He shrugged at the windshield
'Man dat a crazy boogoo
He soun like he say
"dat a nice jump you got too"'

W H (Wystan Hugh) Auden (1907–73)

Auden was born in York and educated at Oxford. He was the leading figure of
a group of poets in the thirties, including Day Lewis, MacNeice, and Spender.
Although his sexual orientation was homosexual, in 1935 he married Erika
Mann, the daughter of the German novelist Thomas Mann, in order to provide
her with a British passport to escape from Nazi Germany. In 1939 he left for
the United States, where he met Chester Kallman, his lifelong friend and
companion. He died at their home in Austria in 1973.

The legendary Greek character Icarus flew too close to the sun, which melted
the wax of his wings; he fell into the sea and drowned. Brueghel's painting 'The
Fall of Icarus' hangs in the Musée des Beaux Arts (Museum of Fine Arts) in
Brussels. It is as Auden describes it in this poem. 'Old Masters' are painters
of earlier centuries.

Musée des Beaux Arts

About suffering they were never wrong,
The Old Masters: how well they understood
Its human position; how it takes place
While someone else is eating or opening a window or just walking dully
    along;
How, when the aged are reverently, passionately waiting
For the miraculous birth, there always must be
Children who do not specially want it to happen, skating
On a pond at the edge of the wood:
They never forgot
That even the dreadful martyrdom must run its course
Anyhow in a corner, some untidy spot
Where the dogs go on with their doggy life and the torturer's horse
Scratches its innocent behind on a tree.

In Brueghel's *Icarus*, for instance: how everything turns away
Quite leisurely from the disaster; the ploughman may
Have heard the splash, the forsaken cry,
But for him it was not an important failure; the sun shone
As it had to on the white legs disappearing into the green
Water; and the expensive delicate ship that must have seen
Something amazing, a boy falling out of the sky,
Had somewhere to get to and sailed calmly on.

Funeral blues

Stop all the clocks, cut off the telephone,
Prevent the dog from barking with a juicy bone,
Silence the pianos and with muffled drum
Bring out the coffin, let the mourners come.

Let aeroplanes circle moaning overhead
Scribbling on the sky the message He Is Dead,
Put crepe bows round the white necks of the public doves,
Let the traffic policemen wear black cotton gloves.

He was my North, my South, my East and West,
My working week and my Sunday rest,
My noon, my midnight, my talk, my song;
I thought love would last for ever: I was wrong.

The stars are not wanted now; put out every one;
Pack up the moon and dismantle the sun;
Pour away the ocean and sweep up the wood;
For nothing now can ever come to any good.

Louis MacNeice (1907–63)

MacNeice was born in Belfast, Northern Ireland, and educated at Oxford. For
a time he lectured in Classics, and then worked in the drama department of the
BBC. He was one of the poets of the thirties who were distinctively left-wing in
their political views.

Prayer before birth

I am not yet born; O hear me.
Let not the bloodsucking bat or the rat or the stoat or the club-
    footed ghoul come near me.

I am not yet born; console me.
I fear that the human race may with tall walls wall me,
    with strong drugs dope me, with wise lies lure me,
        on black racks rack me, in blood-baths roll me.

I am not yet born; provide me
With water to dandle me, grass to grow for me, trees to talk
    to me, sky to sing to me, birds and a white light
        in the back of my mind to guide me.

I am not yet born; forgive me
For the sins that in me the world shall commit, my words
    when they speak me, my thoughts when they think me,
        my treason engendered by traitors beyond me,
            my life when they murder by means of my
                hands, my death when they live me.

I am not yet born; rehearse me
In the parts I must play and the cues I must take when
    old men lecture me, bureaucrats hector me, mountains
        frown at me, lovers laugh at me, the white
            waves call me to folly and the desert calls
                me to doom and the beggar refuses
                    my gift and my children curse me.

I am not yet born; O hear me,
Let not the man who is beast or who thinks he is God
      come near me.

I am not yet born; O fill me
With strength against those who would freeze my
      humanity, would dragoon me into a lethal automaton,
            would make me a cog in a machine, a thing with
                  one face, a thing, and against all those
                  who would dissipate my entirety, would
                        blow me like thistledown hither and
                              thither or hither and thither
                              like water held in the
                                    hands would spill me.

Let them not make me a stone and let them not spill me.
Otherwise kill me.

Stephen Spender (1909–95)

Spender was educated at Oxford, where he met Auden and MacNeice. During
the Spanish Civil War (1936–39) he did propaganda work in Spain for the
Republican cause. He outlived all the other 1930s' poets; and was knighted.

My parents kept me from children who were rough

My parents kept me from children who were rough
Who threw words like stones and who wore torn clothes.
Their thighs showed through rags. They ran in the street
And climbed cliffs and stripped by the country streams.

I feared more than tigers their muscles like iron
Their jerking hands and their knees tight on my arms.
I feared the salt coarse pointing of those boys
Who copied my lisp behind me on the road.

They were lithe, they sprang out behind hedges
Like dogs to bark at my world. They threw mud
While I looked the other way, pretending to smile.
I longed to forgive them, but they never smiled.

Elizabeth Bishop (1911—79)

Bishop was born in Massachusetts in the United States of America, and spent her childhood with her grandparents in Nova Scotia, after her father died and her mother's mental illness led to her being permanently confined. Later she lived with an aunt in Massachusetts and graduated from Vassar College. She travelled to Key West, France, and Mexico; she lived for nineteen years in Brazil. For the last years of her life she taught at Harvard University and lived in Boston.

First death in Nova Scotia

In the cold, cold parlor
my mother laid out Arthur
beneath the chromographs:
Edward, Prince of Wales,
with Princess Alexandra,
and King George with Queen Mary.
Below them on the table
stood a stuffed loon
shot and stuffed by Uncle
Arthur, Arthur's father.

Since Uncle Arthur fired
a bullet into him,
he hasn't said a word.
He kept his own counsel
on his white, frozen lake,
the marble-topped table.
His breast was deep and white,
cold and caressable;
his eyes were red glass,
much to be desired.

'Come,' said my mother,
'Come and say good-bye
to your little cousin Arthur.'
I was lifted up and given
one lily of the valley
to put in Arthur's hand.
Arthur's coffin was

a little frosted cake,
and the red-eyed loon eyed it
from his white, frozen lake.

Arthur was very small.
He was all white, like a doll
that hadn't been painted yet.
Jack Frost had started to paint him
the way he always painted
the Maple Leaf (Forever).
He had just begun on his hair,
a few red strokes, and then
Jack Frost had dropped the brush
and left him white, forever.

The gracious royal couples
were warm in red and ermine;
their feet were well wrapped up
in the ladies' ermine trains.
They invited Arthur to be
the smallest page at court.
But how could Arthur go,
clutching his tiny lily,
with his eyes shut up so tight
and the roads deep in snow?

Seascape

This celestial seascape, with white herons got up as angels,
flying as high as they want and as far as they want sidewise
in tiers and tiers of immaculate reflections;
the whole region, from the highest heron
down to the weightless mangrove island
with bright green leaves edged neatly with bird-droppings
like illumination in silver,
and down to the suggestively Gothic arches of the mangrove roots
and the beautiful pea-green back-pasture
where occasionally a fish jumps, like a wild-flower
in an ornamental spray of spray;

this cartoon by Raphael for a tapestry for a Pope:
it does look like heaven.
But a skeletal lighthouse standing there
in black and white clerical dress,
who lives on his nerves, thinks he knows better.
He thinks that hell rages below his iron feet,
that that is why the shallow water is so warm,
and he knows that heaven is not like this.
Heaven is not like flying or swimming,
but has something to do with blackness and a strong glare
and when it gets dark he will remember something
strongly worded to say on the subject.

Modikwe Dikobe (b 1913)

Dikobe was born in Seabe in what was then the northern Transvaal. At the age
of ten he moved to Johannesburg, left school after Standard 6 (Grade 8), and
worked at various times as a newspaper-seller, a hawker, a clerk, a bookkeeper,
a trade unionist and a night-watchman. In the early 1960s he was detained,
and then banned. In 1977 he retired to a small plot in the countryside.

Grave of unknown whiteman

Rest in peace, old man
A heap of rocks on your grave
Is a token of respect
Bestowed on you.

You chose this part of the country
For a home
On a slope of those rocks
Was your community
And across that road
You sowed corn
And watered your cattle in that pan.

In years of dearth
We shared together
Helped each other in time of need.

Rest in peace, old man
Your kindred are here
Paying due respect
Rest in peace!

Dylan Thomas (1914–53)

Thomas was born in Swansea in Wales, and died in New York while on an
American lecture-tour. He and his wife Caitlin (they had a fiery and passionate
marriage) and their three children settled in the small Welsh fishing village of
Laugharne. He was a fine actor and reader, and managed to complete his radio
play *Under Milk Wood* just before his death from alcohol poisoning.

The hunchback in the park

The hunchback in the park
A solitary mister
Propped between trees and water
From the opening of the garden lock
That lets the trees and water enter
Until the Sunday sombre bell at dark

Eating bread from a newspaper
Drinking water from the chained cup
That the children filled with gravel
In the fountain basin where I sailed my ship
Slept at night in a dog kennel
But nobody chained him up.

Like the park birds he came early
Like the water he sat down
And Mister they called Hey mister
The truant boys from the town
Running when he had heard them clearly
On out of sound

Past lake and rockery
Laughing when he shook his paper
Hunchbacked in mockery
Through the loud zoo of the willow groves

Dodging the park keeper
With his stick that picked up leaves.

And the old dog sleeper
Alone between nurses and swans
While the boys among willows
Made the tigers jump out of their eyes
To roar on the rockery stones
And the groves were blue with sailors

Made all day until bell time
A woman figure without fault
Straight as a young elm
Straight and tall from his crooked bones
That she might stand in the night
After the locks and chains

All night in the unmade park
After the railings and shrubberies
The birds the grass the trees the lake
And the wild boys innocent as strawberries
Had followed the hunchback
To his kennel in the dark.

This next poem was written when Thomas's father was dying. Compare it with Sally-Ann Murray's poem 'For Poppa (1899–983), DSM 1917' (p. 251).

Do not go gentle into that good night

Do not go gentle into that good night,
Old age should burn and rave at close of day;
Rage, rage against the dying of the light.

Though wise men at their end know dark is right,
Because their words had forked no lightning they
Do not go gentle into that good night.

Good men, the last wave by, crying how bright
Their frail deeds might have danced in a green bay,
Rage, rage against the dying of the light.

Wild men who caught and sang the sun in flight,
And learn, too late, they grieved it on its way,
Do not go gentle into that good night.

Grave men, near death, who see with blinding sight
Blind eyes could blaze like meteors and be gay,
Rage, rage against the dying of the light.

And you, my father, there on the sad height,
Curse, bless, me now with your fierce tears, I pray.
Do not go gentle into that good night.
Rage, rage against the dying of the light.

Judith Wright (b 1915)

Wright was born in New South Wales in Australia, and was educated at Sydney
University. She has spent much of her life in the countryside, and conservation
is one of her major preoccupations. More than ten collections of her poems have
appeared over the years.

Request to a year

If the year is meditating a suitable gift,
I should like it to be the attitude
of my great-great-grandmother,
legendary devotee of the arts,

who, having had eight children
and little opportunity for painting pictures,
sat one day on a high rock
beside a river in Switzerland

and from a difficult distance viewed
her second son, balanced on a small ice-floe,
drift down the current towards a waterfall
that struck rock-bottom eighty feet below,

while her second daughter, impeded,
no doubt, by the petticoats of the day,
stretched out a last-hope alpenstock
(which luckily later caught him on his way).

Nothing, it was evident, could be done;
and with the artist's isolating eye
my great-great-grandmother hastily sketched the scene.
The sketch survives to prove the story by.

Year, if you have no Mother's day present planned;
reach back and bring me the firmness of her hand.

Flying-fox on barbed wire

Little nightmare flying-fox
trapped on the cruel barbs of day
has no weapon but a wing
and a tiny scream.
Here's a patch of night, a thing
that looks by daylight like a hoax;
dawn wouldn't let it fly away
with its kin into its dream,
but stabbed with a pin its velvet hand
and hunt it in a hostile land.

Imp from the world of upside-down,
here's some darkness in a bag
to foil your frightened needle-bite.
Now we can untie
from the staring stake of pain
your black claw on its velvet rag.
Scramble, silent, out of the light
and hang by your feet in the kind-leaved tree.
Gargoyle, thief, forget your grief
and go to your country night; and we,
accomplice to day's enemy,
too must forget
that we and the Devil ever met.

Woman to man

The eyeless labourer in the night,
the selfless, shapeless seed I hold,
builds for its resurrection day –
silent and swift and deep from sight
foresees the unimagined light.

This is no child with a child's face;
this has no name to name it by:
yet you and I have known it well.
This is our hunter and our chase,
the third who lay in our embrace.

This is the strength that your arm knows,
the arc of flesh that is my breast,
the precise crystals of our eyes.
This is the blood's wild tree that grows
the intricate and folded rose.

This is the maker and the made;
this is the question and reply;
the blind head butting at the dark,
the blaze of light along the blade.
Oh hold me, for I am afraid.

Anthony Delius (1916–89)

Delius was born in Simon's Town, spent his childhood on a farm in what was then the Transvaal, and worked as a political journalist. He left South Africa to live in the United Kingdom in 1967.

Emerald dove

The Xhosa say
When the emerald dove
Sits sobbing in the bush
She is thinking of the terrible wars
And she cries
My father is dead
My mother is dead
My sisters are dead
My brothers are all dead
And my heart goes
Doem Doem
Doem doem doem doem
doem
doem.

You will want to question the stereotype in the first stanza of the next poem.

The gamblers

The Coloured long-shore fishermen unfurl
their nets beside the chilly and unrested sea,
and in their heads the little dawn-winds whirl
some scraps of gambling, drink and lechery.

Barefoot on withered kelp and broken shell,
they toss big baskets on the brittle turf,
then with a gambler's bitter patience still
slap down their wagering boat upon the surf.

Day flips a golden coin – but they mock it.
With calloused, careless hands they reach
deep down into the sea's capacious pocket
and pile their silver chips upon the beach.

Gwendolyn Brooks (b 1917)

Brooks is one of the earliest female African American writers to be published. A university teacher, she has written a number of novels and collections of poetry. She won the Pulitzer Prize in 1949 for *Annie Allen*.

The bean eaters

They eat beans mostly, this old yellow pair.
Dinner is a casual affair.
Plain chipware on a plain and creaking wood,
Tin flatware.

Two who are Mostly Good.
Two who have lived their day,
But keep on putting on their clothes
And putting things away.

And remembering…
Remembering, with twinklings and twinges,
As they lean over the beans in their rented back room that
    is full of beads and receipts and dolls and clothes,
    tobacco crumbs, vases and fringes.

To be in love

    To be in love
Is to touch things with a lighter hand.

In yourself you stretch, you are well.

You look at things
Through his eyes.
        A Cardinal is red.
        A sky is blue.
Suddenly you know he knows too.
He is not there but
You know you are tasting together
The winter, or light spring weather.

His hand to take your hand is overmuch.
Too much to bear.

You cannot look in his eyes
Because your pulse must not say
What must not be said.

When he
shuts a door –
Is not there –
Your arms are water.

And you are free
With a ghastly freedom.

You are the beautiful half
Of a golden hurt.

You remember and covet his mouth,
To touch, to whisper on.

Oh when to declare
Is certain Death!

Oh when to apprize
Is to mesmerize.

To see fall down, the Column of Gold,
Into the commonest ash.

Robert Lowell (1917–77)

Lowell was born and lived in New England on the east coast of the United States.
A major preoccupation in his poems is his Boston and Maine ancestry. During
the Second World War he was interned as a conscientious objector. Late in life
his opposition to the Vietnam War kept him very much in the public eye. By
then his bouts of manic illness and drug dependency had become very severe.

Terminal days at Beverly Farms

At Beverly Farms, a portly, uncomfortable boulder
bulked in the garden's centre –
an irregular Japanese touch.
After his Bourbon 'old fashioned', Father,
bronzed, breezy, a shade too ruddy,
swayed as if on deck-duty
under his six pointed star-lantern –
last July's birthday present.
He smiled his oval Lowell smile,
he wore his cream gabardine dinner-jacket,
and indigo cummerbund.
His head was efficient and hairless,
his newly dieted figure was vitally trim.

Father and Mother moved to Beverly Farms
to be a two minute walk from the station,
half an hour by train from the Boston doctors.
They had no sea-view,
but sky-blue tracks of the commuters' railroad shone
like a double-barrelled shotgun
through the scarlet late August sumac,
multiplying like cancer
at their garden's border.

Father had had two coronaries.
He still treasured underhand economies,
but his best friend was his little black *Chevie*,
garaged like a sacrificial steer
with gilded hooves,
yet sensationally sober,
and with less side than an old dancing pump.
The local dealer, a 'buccaneer',

had been bribed a 'king's ransom'
to quickly deliver a car without chrome.

Each morning at eight-thirty,
inattentive and beaming,
loaded with his 'calc' and 'trig' books,
his clipper ship statistics,
and his ivory slide-rule,
Father stole off with the *Chevie*
to loaf in the Maritime Museum at Salem.
He called the curator
'the commander of the Swiss Navy'.

Father's death was abrupt and unprotesting.
His vision was still twenty-twenty.
After a morning of anxious, repetitive smiling,
his last words to Mother were:
'I feel awful.'

My Lai, an American offensive, was one of the worst massacres of the Vietnam War.

Women, children, babies, cows, cats

'It was at My Lai or Sonmy or something,
it was this afternoon…We had these orders,
we had all night to think about it –
we was to burn and kill, then there'd be nothing
standing, women, children, babies, cows, cats…
As soon as we hopped the choppers, we started shooting.
I remember…as we was coming up upon one area
in Pinkville, a man with a gun…running – this lady…
Lieutenant LaGuerre said, "Shoot her." I said,
"You shoot her, I don't want to shoot no lady."
She had one foot in the door…When I turned her,
there was this little one-month-year-old baby
I thought was her gun. It kind of cracked me up.'

Robert Dederick (1919–83)

Dederick was born in the United Kingdom, visited Cape Town during the Second World War, and settled in South Africa after the war. He worked as a legal consultant. Two collections of his poems were published.

Read the next poem together with Ruth Miller's poem of the same name (p. 82).

Mantis

Green as an early leaf in Spring
He was, and no less green for being
Caught green-handed on an Autumn day
When puckered browns were everywhere.
My looming shadow held him there
In such a zone of worry as may
Make the least inclined to prayer
Suddenly inclined to pray.
It is improbable of course
That he could take the longer view
Beyond my local whelm of force
And pray in aid some primal Cause
Of whose effects we two were two;
Yet demonstrably there he was,
Clasping each green hand in each –
First in my shadow as if to beseech
And later, when my shadow withdrew,
As if in such thanksgiving mood
As those least given to gratitude
Are not entirely stranger to.

Lawrence Ferlinghetti (b 1919)

Ferlinghetti was born in Yonkers, New York. He was one of the group of poets known as the Beat Poets in the 1950s.

Read this poem side by side with others that are about poetry: Denise Levertov's 'The secret' (p. 98) and Niyi Osundare's 'The poet' (p. 195). Notice how he pinpoints the twin aspirations of 'truth' and 'beauty', just as Keats did at the end of his 'Ode on a Grecian urn' (p. 15).

Constantly risking absurdity

Constantly risking absurdity
                            and death
            whenever he performs
                        above the heads
                                of his audience
        the poet like an acrobat
                        climbs on rime
                                to a high wire of his own making
    and balancing on eyebeams
                            above a sea of faces
            paces his way
                    to the other side of day
        performing entrechats
                        and sleight-of-foot tricks
        and other high theatrics
                        and all without mistaking
any thing
            for what it may not be

        For he's the super realist
                            who must perforce perceive
                taut truth
                        before the taking of each stance or step
        in his supposed advance
                        toward that still higher perch
    where Beauty stands and waits
                        with gravity
                            to start her death-defying leap

And he
        a little charleychaplin man
                        who may or may not catch
            her fair eternal form
                        spreadeagled in the empty air
            of existence.

Ruth Miller (1919–69)

Miller was born in Uitenhage in the Eastern Cape, was brought up in what was then the northern Transvaal, and, after her marriage, lived in Johannesburg. The accidental home death by electrocution of her son, aged 14, clouded the last six years of her life: she wrote nothing for some time, and then produced some of her finest work. She died of cancer. Two volumes of her poems appeared during her lifetime: *The Floating Island* and *Selected Poems*; as well as a posthumous volume, *Ruth Miller: Poems, Prose, Plays*.

Compare the two 'Mantis' poems: this one by Ruth Miller and the one by Robert Dederick (p. 80).

Mantis

He lifts his small hands
To god of nothingness.
Jagged legs stand
On pale green crutches.
The pear-shaped pod
Flanged for flight
All dainty lines
Except the head:
Except the triangle terrible as death.

Responding to his hands, I touched him once.
His minute mouth roared
In such a horror of silence that I saw;
I saw his face grow large as mine
The tender spring green blades of him
Thrust like vengeance. His vicious eyes
Glared. His mouth was red
As hell, the pointed face
Filling with knowledgeable malice.
His hands –
Came for me, crept for me, felt for me through the space
Of cosmic distances that make an inch.

Now that I am brittle as a twig
Time having squeezed the sap and wrung me dry
To the bone, to the outdistancing brain,
Being careful to be quiet and restrained,
Would the terrible triangle of my face
Make *him* afraid?

It is better to be together

It is better to be
Together. Tossed together
In a white wave, than to see
The ocean like an eagle.

It is better to lie
In the stormy seething
Than to judge the weather
In an eagle's eye.

Cold is the bird
Who flies too far
In the clear vision
Which saints and eagles share:
Their faraway eyes are bitter
With darkened prayer.

O, it is better to try
With the white wave, together
To overturn the sky.

May Swenson (1919–89)

Swenson was born in Utah in the United States, and lived in New York.
In 1980 she was appointed as chancellor of the Academy of American Poets.
She published many collections of poems over the years.

The key to everything

Is there anything I can do
or has everything been done
or do
you prefer somebody else to do
it or don't
you trust me to do
it right or is it hopeless and no one can do
a thing or do
you suppose I don't
really want to do
it and am just saying that or don't
you hear me at all or what?

You're
waiting for
the right person the doctor or
the nurse the father or
the mother or
the person with the name you keep
mumbling in your sleep
that no one ever heard of there's no one
named that really
except yourself maybe

If I knew what the name was I'd
prove it's your own name
twisted in some way the one you
keep mumbling but you
won't tell me your
name or
don't you know it
yourself that's it
of course you've
forgotten or
never quite knew it or
weren't willing to believe it

Then there *is* something I
can do I
can find your name for you
that's the key to everything once you'd
repeat it clearly you'd
come awake you'd
get up and walk knowing where you're
going where you
came from

And you'd
love me
after that or would you
hate me?
no once you'd
get there you'd

remember and love me
of course I'd
be gone by then I'd
be far away

Tatamkhulu Afrika (b 1920)

Afrika was born in Egypt and brought up in South Africa. He served with the
South African forces in North Africa during the Second World War, was captured
at Tobruk, and spent three years as a prisoner of war in Italy and Germany. Back
in Southern Africa, he was, at various times, a shop assistant, an auditor's clerk,
a barman, a drummer in a band, and a miner in the Namibian copper mines.
In 1964 he converted to Islam and founded the Al-Jihaad organization, which
campaigned against the National Party government's declaration of District Six
as a white area; this led to his arrest. As an underground member of Umkhonto
we Sizwe, he was again arrested in 1987, at the age of 66, and was banned from
writing and speaking in public for five years. He has published a number of
collections of poems, as well as some works of fiction.

The prisoner

I am sentenced.
The court orderly's hand falls heavily on my arm.
What does he fear,
that I will flee screaming down the corridors,
leap on an unsuspecting magistrate,
bleed on the court's floors?
We file past my friends,
so pitifully few.
All huddled up together on a single front bench,
their heads hang.
Why can't they look at me?
Is it from pity or are they now
the bearers of the guilt I cannot feel?
We go down to the cavern beneath the courts:
keys jangle, doors clang,
someone shuffles past in leg-irons;
incongruously, someone sings.
It is an abattoir where no blood runs,
a stockyard where silence crawls,

cowering, into little corners
and hangs there, belly soft
beneath the searching hand.
They take my fingerprints, again,
saying, 'Relax, relax,'
as they roll the limp, lifeless finger
on the still living hand
lovingly across the scarring pad.
Then they show me to a wash-basin,
cracked and stained,
and a little tin of scouring powder,
caked as hard as stone,
saying, 'Wash, wash,'
but not unkindly so,
just absently, as though I wasn't really there.
Am I really here?
They take me to a cell.
I am alone,
graffiti on the walls:
what else?
I have read it all before.
A toilet-bowl without a seat:
I sit on it and drop my faeces quickly,
not knowing how long I will be
the only one here.
Shitting in the round
is such a very animal thing:
am I still a man?
Thin as a gold hair,
a tendril of bright sunlight cracks the wall.
How high are the bars,
but still they snatch a little patch of blue
and somewhere a bird is singing,
or so I pretend.
I am alone.
Am I alone?
Who is the stranger sitting in the corner then?
The sunlight does not touch his face.
Though I turn and turn,
he wears a shadow like a veil,
but the bright eyes, gleaming through it,

question mine,
and I feel that I yet will come to know him well,
as I should have known him all along,
but this is the first time I have sat with him,
measuring him as he is measuring me,
listening to freedom wailing at the wall…

The beggar

When I passed
the bus-stop, his black
as biltong hand
thrust out,
demanding alms.
Beneath the grime,
he was a yellow man,
and small,
and crumpled as a towel,
eyes receding into bone,
shivering, too thin frame
denying the truculence of the hand.
'No,' I said,
and walked on,
annoyed that I was annoyed,
swatting off shame
all the way into town.
Coming back,
the day-long drizzle stopped
and a suddenly clear
sky sang
of summer round the bend,
white sails in the Bay,
birds grown garrulous again.
I looked for him.
He was lying on his back in the sun,
eyes closed,
stretched out long as a spill,
hardly distinguishable
from any of the other
drifts of debris in the lane.

'Drunk again,' I thought,
and paused, then pressed
my penance into his palm.
Quick as a trap,
his fingers lashed
over it: surprised
sober eyes blessed
me for being kind.
Then he slept again,
fist wrapped, tight,
about the bribe my guilt refused,
limbs thrown wide
as though a car had flung him there
and left him to a healing of the sun.

Oodgeroo of the tribe Noonuccal (1920–93)

Oodgeroo was formerly known as Kath Walker. She was born on Stradbroke
Island off the Queensland coast in Australia. She was of the tribe Noonuccal,
and her totem was the carpet snake. She left school at 13 to go into domestic
service in Brisbane. She was in the Women's Army Service during the Second
World War. After the war, she became very much involved in Aboriginal rights,
as well as leading an educational and cultural centre on Stradbroke Island. The
first of several volumes of her poetry was published in 1964.

Oodgeroo gave this note to the following poem: 'Willie Mackenzie was a full-
blood Aboriginal, the last surviving member of the Darwarbada tribe of the
Caboolture district. He died in 1968, age unknown but probably in the eighties.
His tribal name was Geerbo, his totem the native bee. The "Mackenzie" came
from his family's first white boss, a selector of that name.'

Last of his tribe

Change is the law. The new must oust the old.
I look at you and am back in the long ago,
Old pinnaroo lonely and lost here,
Last of your clan.
Left only with your memories, you sit
And think of the gay throng, the happy people,
The voices and the laughter
All gone, all gone,
And you remain alone.

I asked and you let me hear
The soft vowelly tongue to be heard now
No more for ever. For me
You enact old scenes, old ways, you who have used
Boomerang and spear.
You singer of ancient tribal songs,
You leader once in the corroboree,
You twice in fierce tribal fights
With wild enemy blacks from over the river,
All gone, all gone. And I feel
The sudden sting of tears, Willie Mackenzie
In the Salvation Army Home.
Displaced person in your own country,
Lonely in teeming city crowds,
Last of your tribe.

Acacia Ridge

White men, turn quickly the earth of Acacia Ridge,
Hide the evidence lying there
Of the black race evicted as of old their fathers were;
Cover up the crime committed this day,
Call it progress, the white man's way.

Take no heed of the pregnant black woman in despair
As with her children she has to go;
Ignore her bitter tears that unheeded flow;
While her children cling to her terrified
Bulldozers huddle the crime aside.

White men, turn quickly the earth of Acacia Ridge,
Plough the guilt in, cover and hide the shame;
These are black and so without right to blame
As bulldozers brutally drive, ruthless and sure
Through and over the poor homes of the evicted poor.

Homeless now they stand and watch as the rain pours down;
This is the justice brought to the black man there,
Injustice which to whites you would never dare,
You whites with all the power and privilege
Who committed the crime of Acacia Ridge.

Gabriel Okara (b 1921)

Okara was born in Nembe in the Ijaw district of Nigeria. He became a printer
and bookbinder. Later he studied journalism at Northwestern University in the
United States. He supported the Biafran cause during the Nigerian civil war.
He is well known for his 1964 novel *The Voice*. Several of his poems explore the
differences between African and Western cultures.

The term 'inside' is Okara's rendering of an expression from his native Ijaw. It
appears in many of his poems, and represents the sum total of the human being.

You laughed and laughed and laughed

In your ears my song
is motor car misfiring
stopping with a choking cough;
and you laughed and laughed and laughed.

In your eyes my ante-
natal walk was inhuman, passing
your 'omnivorous understanding'
and you laughed and laughed and laughed.

You laughed at my song,
you laughed at my walk.

Then I danced my magic dance
to the rhythm of talking
drums pleading, but you shut your
eyes and laughed and laughed and laughed.

And then I opened my mystic
inside wide like
the sky, instead you entered your
car and laughed and laughed and laughed.

You laughed at my dance,
you laughed at my inside.

You laughed and laughed and laughed
But your laughter was ice-block
laughter and it froze your inside froze
your voice froze your ears
froze your eyes and froze your tongue.

And now it's my turn to laugh;
but my laughter is not
ice-block laughter. For I
know not cars, know not ice-blocks.

My laughter is the fire
of the eye of the sky, the fire
of the earth, the fire of the air,
the fire of the seas and the
rivers fishes animals trees
and it thawed your inside,
thawed your voice, thawed your
ears, thawed your eyes and
thawed your tongue.

So a meek wonder held
your shadow and you whispered:
'Why so?'
And I answered:
'Because my fathers and I
are owned by the living
warmth of the earth
through our naked feet.'

Okara tells us that the Aladuras are 'a Christian sect addicted to ritual bathing'.
'Highlife' is a distinctive West African popular music. Cowrie shells are used in
West African religious practice as oracles interpreted by the seers, the 'Babalawo'.
Because of their common concerns with religion, traditional or past beliefs, and
the sea, compare Okara's poem with Matthew Arnold's 'Dover Beach' (p. 23).

One night at Victoria Beach

The wind comes rushing from the sea,
the waves curling like mambas strike
the sands and recoiling hiss in rage
washing the Aladuras' feet pressing hard
on the sand and with eyes fixed hard
on what only hearts can see, they shouting
pray, the Aladuras pray; and coming
from booths behind, compelling highlife
forces ears; and car lights startle pairs
arm in arm passing washer-words back
and forth like haggling sellers and buyers –

Still they pray, the Aladuras pray
with hands pressed against their hearts
and their white robes pressed against
their bodies by the wind; and drinking
palmwine and beer, the people boast
at bars at the beach. Still they pray.

They pray, the Aladuras pray
to what only hearts can see while dead
fishermen long dead with bones rolling
nibbled clean by nibbling fishes, follow
four dead cowries shining like stars
into deep sea where fishes sit in judgement;
and living fishermen in dark huts
sit round dim lights with Babalawo
throwing their souls in four cowries
on sand, trying to see tomorrow.

Still, they pray, the Aladuras pray
to what only hearts can see behind
the curling waves and the sea, the stars
and the subduing unanimity of the sky
and their white bones beneath the sand.

And standing dead on dead sands,
I felt my knees touch living sands –
but the rushing wind killed the budding words.

Philip Larkin (1922–85)

Larkin was born in Coventry and educated at Oxford. He spent all his adult life working as a librarian, achieving a considerable reputation as the head librarian at Hull University. He enjoyed the companionship of Monica Jones (whom he met when she was an English lecturer at Leicester University while he was the librarian there) for thirty-eight years. While he had a wicked sense of humour, he was by all accounts a difficult and sometimes not very likeable personality.

Coming

On longer evenings,
Light, chill and yellow,
Bathes the serene
Foreheads of houses.
A thrush sings,
Laurel-surrounded
In the deep bare garden,
Its fresh-peeled voice
Astonishing the brickwork.
It will be spring soon,
It will be spring soon –
And I, whose childhood
Is a forgotten boredom,
Feel like a child
Who comes on a scene
Of adult reconciling,
And can understand nothing
But the unusual laughter,
And starts to be happy.

The 'young lady' in the next poem was not Monica Jones, but Winifred Arnott, a young librarian with whom Larkin had a casual flirtation while they both worked at the library of Queen's University in Belfast, Northern Ireland. He kept the photograph he pinched all his life; it is reproduced in his biography, published after his death.

Lines on a young lady's photograph album

At last you yielded up the album, which,
Once open, sent me distracted. All your ages
Matt and glossy on the thick black pages!
Too much confectionery, too rich:
I choke on such nutritious images.

My swivel eye hungers from pose to pose –
In pigtails, clutching a reluctant cat;
Or furred yourself, a sweet girl-graduate;
Or lifting a heavy-headed rose
Beneath a trellis, or in a trilby hat

(Faintly disturbing, that, in several ways) –
From every side you strike at my control,
Not least through these disquieting chaps who loll
At ease about your earlier days:
Not quite your class, I'd say, dear, on the whole.

But o, photography! as no art is,
Faithful and disappointing! that records
Dull days as dull, and hold-it smiles as frauds,
And will not censor blemishes
Like washing-lines, and Hall's-Distemper boards,

But shows the cat as disinclined, and shades
A chin as doubled when it is, what grace
Your candour thus confers upon her face!
How overwhelmingly persuades
That this is a real girl in a real place,

In every sense empirically true!
Or is it just *the past*? Those flowers, that gate,
These misty parks and motors, lacerate
Simply by being over; you
Contract my heart by looking out of date.

Yes, true; but in the end, surely, we cry
Not only at exclusion, but because
It leaves us free to cry. We know *what was*
Won't call on us to justify
Our grief, however hard we yowl across

The gap from eye to page. So I am left
To mourn (without a chance of consequence)
You, balanced on a bike against a fence;
To wonder if you'd spot the theft
Of this one of you bathing; to condense

In short, a past that no one now can share,
No matter whose your future; calm and dry,
It holds you like a heaven, and you lie
Unvariably lovely there,
Smaller and clearer as the years go by.

Link up what Larkin says in the next poem, written in 1954, with Matthew
Arnold's ideas on the loss of faith in 'Dover Beach' (p. 23), written almost ninety
years earlier, in 1867.

Church going

Once I am sure there's nothing going on
I step inside, letting the door thud shut.
Another church: matting, seats, and stone,
And little books; sprawlings of flowers, cut
For Sunday, brownish now; some brass and stuff
Up at the holy end; the small neat organ;
And a tense, musty, unignorable silence,
Brewed God knows how long. Hatless, I take off
My cycle-clips in awkward reverence,

Move forward, run my hand around the font.
From where I stand, the roof looks almost new –
Cleaned, or restored? Someone would know: I don't.
Mounting the lectern, I peruse a few
Hectoring large-scale verses, and pronounce
'Here endeth' much more loudly than I'd meant.
The echoes snigger briefly. Back at the door
I sign the book, donate an Irish sixpence,
Reflect the place was not worth stopping for.

Yet stop I did: in fact I often do,
And always end much at a loss like this,
Wondering what to look for; wondering, too,
When churches fall completely out of use
What we shall turn them into, if we shall keep
A few cathedrals chronically on show,
Their parchment, plate and pyx in locked cases,
And let the rest rent-free to rain and sheep.
Shall we avoid them as unlucky places?

Or, after dark, will dubious women come
To make their children touch a particular stone;
Pick simples for a cancer; or on some
Advised night see walking a dead one?
Power of some sort or other will go on
In games, in riddles, seemingly at random;

But superstition, like belief, must die,
And what remains when disbelief has gone?
Grass, weedy pavement, brambles, buttress, sky,

A shape less recognisable each week,
A purpose more obscure. I wonder who
Will be the last, the very last, to seek
This place for what it was; one of the crew
That tap and jot and know what rood-lofts were?
Some ruin-bibber, randy for antique,
Or Christmas-addict, counting on a whiff
Of gowns-and-bands and organ-pipes and myrrh?
Or will he be my representative,

Bored, uninformed, knowing the ghostly silt
Dispersed, yet tending to this cross of ground
Through suburb scrub because it held unspilt
So long and equably what since is found
Only in separation – marriage, and birth,
And death, and thoughts of these – for which was built
This special shell? For, though I've no idea
What this accoutred frowsty barn is worth,
It pleases me to stand in silence here;

A serious house on serious earth it is,
In whose blent air all our compulsions meet,
Are recognised, and robed as destinies.
And that much never can be obsolete,
Since someone will forever be surprising
A hunger in himself to be more serious,
And gravitating with it to this ground,
Which, he once heard, was proper to grow wise in,
If only that so many dead lie round.

Ambulances

Closed like confessionals, they thread
Loud noons of cities, giving back
None of the glances they absorb.
Light glossy grey, arms on a plaque,
They come to rest at any kerb:
All streets in time are visited.

Then children strewn on steps or road,
Or women coming from the shops
Past smells of different dinners, see
A wild white face that overtops
Red stretcher-blankets momently
As it is carried in and stowed,

And sense the solving emptiness
That lies just under all we do,
And for a second get it whole,
So permanent and blank and true.
The fastened doors recede. *Poor soul,*
They whisper at their own distress;

For borne away in deadened air
May go the sudden shut of loss
Round something nearly at an end,
And what cohered in it across
The years, the unique random blend
Of families and fashions, there

At last begin to loosen. Far
From the exchange of love to lie
Unreachable inside a room
The traffic parts to let go by
Brings closer what is left to come,
And dulls to distance all we are.

David Holbrook (b 1923)

Holbrook was born in Norwich in the United Kingdom. Much of his written
work has related to drama and theatre for young people.

Fingers in the door

For Kate

Careless for an instant I closed my child's fingers in the jamb. She
Held her breath, contorted the whole of her being, foetus-wise, against the
Burning fact of the pain. And for a moment
I wished myself dispersed, in a hundred thousand pieces
Among the dead bright stars. The child's cry broke,

She clung to me, and it crowded in to me how she and I were
Light-years from any mutual help or comfort. For her I cast seed
Into her mother's womb; cells grew and launched itself as a being:
Nothing restores her to my being, or ours, even to the mother who
        within her
Carried and quickened, bore, and sobbed at her separation, despite all
        my envy,
Nothing can restore. She, I, mother, sister, dwell dispersed among dead
        bright stars:
We are there in our hundred thousand pieces!

Denise Levertov (b 1923)

Levertov was born in the United Kingdom of a Russian Jewish father and a Welsh
mother. She served as a nurse during the Second World War, then she married an
American and emigrated to the United States in 1948. She has lectured at many
American universities, and has published numerous collections of poems.

Read this poem together with others concerning poetry: Lawrence
Ferlinghetti's 'Constantly risking absurdity' (p. 81) and Niyi Osundare's
'The poet' (p. 195).

The secret

Two girls discover
the secret of life
in a sudden line of
poetry.

I who don't know the
secret wrote
the line. They
told me

(through a third person)
they had found it

but not what it was,
not even
what line it was. No doubt
by now, more than a week
later, they have forgotten
the secret,

the line, the name of
the poem. I love them
for finding what
I can't find,

and for loving me
for the line I wrote,
and for forgetting it
so that

a thousand times, till death
finds them, they may
discover it again, in other
lines,

in other
happenings. And for
wanting to know it,
for

assuming there is
such a secret, yes,
for that
most of all.

Adolf Eichmann was the chief of Hitler's Gestapo police who was responsible for
sending many thousands of Jewish people to their deaths before and during the
Second World War. He was tried in Israel as a Nazi war criminal in 1961, and
hanged in 1962. The author gives this note to the following poem: 'This poem
is based on the earliest mention, during the trial, of this incident. In a later
statement it was said that the fruit was cherries, that the boy was already in the
garden, doing forced labour, when he was accused of taking the fruit, and that
Eichmann killed him in a tool shed, not beneath the tree. The poem therefore is
not to be taken as a report of what happened but of what I envisioned.' Notice
the use Levertov makes of both colour and taste in the poem.

From *During the Eichmann trial*
The peachtree

The Danube orchards
are full of fruit
but in the city one tree
haunts a boy's dreams

a tree in a villa garden
the Devil's garden
a peach tree

and of its fruit one peach
calls to him

he sees it yellow and ripe
the vivid blood
bright in its round cheek

Next day he knows
he cannot withstand desire
it is no common fruit

it holds some secret
it speaks to the yellow star within him

he scales the wall
enters the garden of death
takes the peach
and death pounces

mister death who rushes out
from his villa
mister death who loves yellow

who wanted that yellow peach
for himself
mister death who signs papers
then eats

telegraphs simply: Shoot them
then eats
mister death who orders
more transports
then eats

he would have enjoyed
the sweetest of all the peaches on his tree
with sour-cream
with brandy

Son of David
's blood, vivid red

and trampled juice
yellow and sweet
flow together beneath the tree

there is more blood than
sweet juice
always more blood – mister
death goes indoors
exhausted

James Baldwin (1924–87)

Baldwin was born in Harlem, New York. An illegitimate child, he had a harsh upbringing under his preacher stepfather. At the age of 15 he himself became a boy-preacher (a 'Young Minister') in the Pentecostal Church; he broke entirely with the church a few years later. At the age of 24 he went to Paris for two years, and thereafter visited Europe often, eventually settling in France for the last years of his life. In the 1960s Baldwin became very much involved in the civil rights movement and was considered the major commentator on African American affairs. He himself moved from supporting Martin Luther King to endorsing the more radical Malcolm X and, after him, the Black Panther movement. His first novel *Go Tell It on the Mountain*, published when he was 29, gives a vivid picture of African American life in the Harlem of the 1930s and 1940s. His second novel *Giovanni's Room* was set in Paris. His other major works include *Notes of a Native Son*, *Another Country*, *The Fire Next Time*, and the play *Blues for Mr Charlie*.

Song (for Skip) section 2

My beloved brother,
I know your walk
and love to hear you
talk that talk
while your furrowed brow
grows young with wonder,
like a small boy, staring at the thunder.

I see you, somehow,
about the age of ten,
determined to enter the world of men,
yet, not too far from your mother's lap,
wearing your stunning
baseball cap.

Perhaps, then, around eleven,
wondering what to take as given,
and, not much later, going through
the agony bequeathed to you.

Then, spun around, then going under,
the small boy staring at the thunder.

Then, take it all
and use it well

this manhood, calculating
through this hell.

James Berry (b 1924)

Berry was born in Jamaica, has lived in the United States, and, since 1945,
in the United Kingdom. Since his first book *Fractured Circles* he has published
a number of collections of his poems. He has also compiled two important
anthologies of West Indian-British poetry.

White child meets black man

She caught me outside a London
suburban shop, I like a giraffe
and she a mouse. I tried to go
but felt she stood
lovely as light on my back.

I turned with hello
and waited. Her eyes got
wider but not her lips.
Hello I smiled again and watched.

She stepped around me
slowly, in a kind of dance,
her wide eyes searching
inch by inch up and down:
no fur no scales no feathers
no shell. Just a live silhouette,
wild and strange
and compulsive
till mother came horrified.

'Mummy is his tummy black?'
Mother grasped her and swung
toward the crowd. She tangled
mother's legs looking back at me.
As I watched them birds were singing.

Dennis Brutus (b 1924)

Brutus was born in Harare (then Salisbury) of South African parents. He was
brought up in South Africa, and educated at the Universities of Fort Hare and
the Witwatersrand. He was a teacher and sports administrator. In 1963 he was
arrested, but escaped while on bail. When re-arrested, he made a further escape
attempt but was shot in the back and subsequently sentenced to imprisonment
on Robben Island. While in prison he wrote some of the finest prison poems to
come out of South Africa. After his release he went into exile in the United
States, where he has taught at a number of universities.

Letters to Martha 4

Particularly in a single cell,
but even in the sections
the religious sense asserts itself;

perhaps a childhood habit of nightly prayers
the accessibility of Bibles,
or awareness of the proximity of death:

and, of course, it is a currency –
pietistic expressions can purchase favours
and it is a way of suggesting reformation
(which can procure promotion);

and the resort of the weak
is to invoke divine revenge
against a rampaging injustice;

but in the grey silence of the empty afternoons
it is not uncommon
to find oneself talking to God.

Letters to Martha 9

The not-knowing
is perhaps the worst part of the agony
for those outside;

not knowing what cruelties must be endured
what indignities the sensitive spirit must face
what wounds the mind can be made to inflict
     on itself;

and the hunger to be thought of
to be remembered
and to reach across space
with filaments of tenderness
and consolation.

And knowledge,
even when it is knowledge of ugliness
seems to be preferable,
can be better endured.

And so,
for your consolation
I send these fragments,
random pebbles I pick up
from the landscape of my own experience,
traversing the same arid wastes
in a montage of glimpses
I allow myself
or stumble across.

Letters to Martha 10

It is not all terror
and deprivation,
you know;

one comes to welcome the closer contact
and understanding one achieves
with one's fellow-men,
fellows, compeers;

and the discipline does much to force
a shape and pattern on one's daily life
as well as on the days

and honest toil
offers some redeeming hours
for the wasted years;

so there are times
when the mind is bright and restful
though alive:
rather like the full calm morning sea.

Nissim Ezekiel (b 1924)

Ezekiel was born in Mumbai (Bombay), India, of Jewish Indian parents, who
were both English- and Marathi-speaking. He was educated at a Catholic school
in Mumbai, and then at Wilson College, Mumbai, and Birbeck College, London.
He has taught at various universities, and was Professor of English Literature at
the University of Bombay from 1972 to his retirement in 1985. His first collection
of poems was published in 1952. Many other collections have followed, and his
Collected Poems was published in 1988. He is acknowledged as India's best-
known English-language poet.

In the next poem, 'goonda' means dirty, and 'lassi' means buttermilk.

The patriot

I am standing for peace and non-violence.
Why world is fighting fighting
Why all people of world
Are not following Mahatma Gandhi,
I am simply not understanding.
Ancient Indian Wisdom is 100% correct.
I should say even 200% correct.
But Modern generation is neglecting –
Too much going for fashion and foreign thing.

Other day I'm reading in newspaper
(Every day I'm reading Times of India
To improve my English Language)
How one goonda fellow
Throw stone at Indirabehn.
Must be student unrest fellow, I am thinking.

Friends, Romans, Countrymen, I am saying (to myself)
Lend me the ears.
Everything is coming –
Regeneration, Remuneration, Contraception.
Be patiently, brothers and sisters.

You want one glass lassi?
Very good for digestion.
With little salt lovely drink,
Better than wine;
Not that I am ever tasting the wine.
I'm the total teetotaller, completely total.
But I say
Wine is for the drunkards only.

What you think of prospects of world peace?
Pakistan behaving like this,
China behaving like that,
It is making me very sad, I am telling you.
Really, most harassing me.
All men are brothers, no?
In India also
Gujaraties, Maharashtrians, Hindiwallahs
All brothers –
Though some are having funny habits.
Still, you tolerate me,
I tolerate you,
One day Ram Rajya is surely coming.

You are going?
But you will visit again
Any time, any day,
I am not believing in ceremony.
Always I am enjoying your company.

Sydney Clouts (1926–82)

Clouts was born in Cape Town and attended the University of Cape Town. He
served in the South African forces during World War Two. He left South Africa
in 1961 to live in the United Kingdom. In 1966 his first collection of poems *One
Life* was awarded both the Ingrid Jonker and Olive Schreiner Prizes. His
Collected Poems was published in 1984.

Karroo stop

A whole
trainful of coal
like a soul
burnt black in a hole
or tunnel, passed us slowly.
We were halted in our carriage. The roll,
roll, roll, roll, roll, roll, roll,
dragged painfully, each truck like the goal
achieved, yet still this kept control
of each eye.

A horse and a foal
beyond were meagre to it, coal-
black horse and foal,
and far-off clouds stroll white
in little mounds, and the coal
in mounds and piles that crawl
and crawl.

A sigh, a grunt from us all,
with one exception: I saw patrol
like a mole
underground, through walls
of skewer patience, cold and fire,
an old old
man's sharp smile, an old
man wrinkled small
with teeth like coal.

Elizabeth Jennings (b 1926)

Jennings was born in Lincolnshire, and educated at Oxford. She is an established
British writer, from her first volume of poems *Recoveries* in 1964, through to her
Collected Poems.

For a child born dead

What ceremony can we fit
You into now? If you had come
Out of a warm and noisy room

To this, there'd be an opposite
For us to know you by. We could
Imagine you in lively mood.

And then look at the other side,
The mood drawn out of you, the breath
Defeated by the power of death.
But we have never seen you stride
Ambitiously the world we know.
You could not come and yet you go.

But there is nothing now to mar
Your clear refusal of our world.
Not in our memories can we mould
You or distort your character.
Then all our consolation is
That grief can be as pure as this.

One flesh

Lying apart now, each in a separate bed,
He with a book, keeping the light on late,
She like a girl dreaming of childhood,
All men elsewhere – it is as if they wait
Some new event: the book he holds unread,
Her eyes fixed on the shadows overhead.

Tossed up like flotsam from a former passion,
How cool they lie. They hardly ever touch,
Or if they do it is like a confession
Of having little feeling – or too much.
Chastity faces them, a destination
For which their whole lives were a preparation.

Strangely apart, yet strangely close together,
Silence between them like a thread to hold
And not wind in. And time itself's a feather
Touching them gently. Do they know they're old,
These two who are my father and my mother
Whose fire from which I came, has now grown cold?

Bernard Kops (b 1926)

Kops was born and lives in the United Kingdom. He is best known for his plays set in the East End of London.

Shalom bomb

I want a bomb, my own private bomb, my shalom bomb.
I'll test it in the morning, when my son awakes,
hot and stretching, smelling beautiful from sleep. Boom! Boom!
Come my son dance naked in the room.
I'll test it on the landing and wake my neighbours,
the masons and the whores and the students who live downstairs.

Oh I must have a bomb and I'll throw open windows and
count down as I whizz around the living room,
on his bike with him flying angels on my shoulder,
and my wife dancing in her dressing gown.

I want a happy family bomb, a do-it-yourself bomb,
I'll climb on the roof and ignite it there about noon.
My improved design will gong the world and we'll all eat lunch.

My pretty little bomb will play a daytime lullaby and
thank you bomb for now my son falls fast asleep.
My love come close, close, the curtains, my lovely bomb, my darling,
my naughty bomb. Burst around us, burst between us, burst within
us. Light up the universe, then linger, linger
while the drone of the world recedes.

Shalom Bomb –

I want to explode the breasts of my wife. Ping! Ping!
In the afternoon and wake everyone,
to explode over playgrounds and parks, just as children
come from schools. I want a laughter bomb,
filled with sherbet fountains, liquorice allsorts, chocolate kisses,
candy floss,
tinsel and streamers, balloons and fireworks, lucky bags,
bubbles and masks and false noses.
I want my bomb to sprinkle the earth with roses.

I want the streets of the world to be filled with crammed, jammed
kids, screaming with laughter, pointing their hands with wonder,
at my lemonade ice-cream lightning and mouthorgan thunder.
I want a one-man-band bomb. My own bomb.
My live long and die happy bomb, my die peacefully old age bomb,
in our own beds, bomb.
My Om Mane Padme Hum bomb, my Tiddley Om Pom bomb,
my goodnight bomb, my sleeptight bomb,
my see you in the morning bomb,
I want my bomb, my own private bomb, my Shalom Bomb.

Taufiq Rafat (b 1927)

Rafat was born in Sialkot in what became Pakistan. He started writing poems
when he was twelve. He has also written plays in English. His poems have
frequently been anthologized.

The squalor in which some people live

The squalor in which some people live
Disgusts me, and when I see a man
Urinating on the road, it makes me mad.

Dear God, have I forgotten so soon
My own beginnings?

         The oblique house
In Shahalam where my mother was born
Is no longer there; in its place
Stands a dry fountain, a symbol of
The act that severed a continent.
But it inflames the eye of memory
Like a mote: room piled upon room,
And not a ventilator anywhere
To let the stale air out. Down one side
A gutter ran like a sore; the other
Shared with a Hindu dealer in brass.

My grandfather, splendidly moustached,
Boisterous, semi-naked, who turned
From mashing bones to mending them,
The most skilful bone-setter of his day,

With a certificate from Lord Kitchener
To prove it, still young at eighty,
Held court on the ground-floor, surrounded
By the appurtenances of his trade
And the patients' relatives. I can see him
Cajoling a wayward bone into place
Cannily aided by a burst of invective
So fierce, it makes me shudder still.
As we stood by at a respectful distance
Memorizing his words, he pointed us out
To his neighbours proudly as the children
Of a millionaire, hastily adding,
Of course, he did not care a damn.

In that smell of oil and lint and dung
And unaired quilts, how carefree we were,
For a few ecstatic weeks each winter
Like the barna tree, all flower
And no leaf. The filth was part of us,
As we grew tall in that time of love.

The hands of the clock in moving forward
Are moving back. The family business
Slides downwards imperceptibly
While I bandy words in a foreign tongue.

Circumcision

Having hauled down my pyjamas
they dragged me, all legs and teeth,
that fateful afternoon, to a stool
before which the barber hunkered
with an open cut-throat. He stropped it
on his palm with obvious relish.
I did not like his mustachios, nor
his conciliatory smile. Somehow
they made me sit, and two cousins
held a leg apiece. The barber
looked at me; I stared right back,
defying him to start something.
He just turned aside to whisper
to my cousin who suddenly cried

'oh look at that golden bird',
and being only six I looked up;
which was all the time he needed
to separate me from my prepuce.
'Bastard, sonofapig,' I roared,
'sister-ravisher, you pimp
and catamite,' while he applied
salve and bandaged the organ.
Beside myself with indignation
and pain, I forgot the presence
of elders, and cursed and cursed
in the graphic vocabulary
of the lanes, acquired at leap-frog,
marbles, and blindman's buff.
Still frothing at the mouth they fetched
me to bed, where an anxious mother
kissed and consoled me. It was not
till I was alone that I dared
to look down at my naked middle.
When I saw it so foreshortened,
raw, and swathed in lint, I burst
into fresh tears. Dismally
I wondered if I would ever
be able to pee again.

                        This
was many many years ago.
I have since learnt it was more
than a ritual, for by the act
of a pull and downward slash,
they prepare us for the disappointments
at the absence of golden birds
life will ask us to look at
between our circumcision and death.

Lionel Abrahams (b 1928)

Abrahams was born in Johannesburg, and has lived there all his life. Physically
disabled from birth, he has lived an extremely active life as a writer, critic, editor
and mentor to many writers. In the early 1970s he founded Renoster Books,
which published the first three volumes of black South African poetry in English:
Mbuyiseni Oswald Mtshali's *Sounds of a Cowhide Drum*, Mongane Wally Serote's

Yakhal'inkomo, and an anthology of various writers. He has had four collections of verse published, as well as a novel and a volume of selected writing.

The whiteman blues

Two cars, three loos, a swimming pool,
Investment paintings, kids at a private school...
we entertain with shows or gourmet food –
and yet we don't feel right, we don't feel good.

Why doesn't the having help?
Why doesn't the spending save?
Why doesn't the fun –
Why doesn't the culture –
Why don't the ads add up to something?

We can afford to say we know
the blacks are really given hell,
Big Boss is harsh and stupid and must go:
we say it – and it helps like one Aspro.
We still feel jumpy, mixed up, not quite well.

Which specialist can cure the thing we've got –
the got-it, gotta-get-it blues,
the deep-freeze, cheaper wholesale, world excursion blues?
We're high on the know-all-about-it booze.
We're bursting with kwashiorkor of the bank.
We're depressed by the whiteman blues.

In the backyards they pray for us.
In Soweto they see our plight.
In the border areas they understand.
In the Bantustans they wait
to pat our shoulder, hold our hand.
They know, they know,
to them it isn't news:
we've got these lost-man, late-man,
money-man, superman,
whiteman blues.

Celebration

Thalia naked, two next week,
runs up the passage toward
me in my wheelchair,
laughs, turns, runs down,
then up and down again, again,
greeting approach each time
with glee. The joke holds even
when someone big brushes through
and Thalia, staggering against the air,
raises hands to ward off wall or fall.
I feel safe for a thousand years.

Maya Angelou (b 1928)

Angelou was born in St Louis, Missouri, in the United States. She has told the
story of her difficult childhood in the autobiographical *I Know Why the Caged
Bird Sings*. She has been a writer, singer, actor, dancer, black activist, editor and
mother. She now holds a lifetime appointment as Professor of American Studies
at Wake Forest University in North Carolina.

On aging

When you see me sitting quietly,
Like a sack left on the shelf,
Don't think I need your chattering,
I'm listening to myself.
Hold! Stop! Don't pity me!
Hold! Stop your sympathy!
Understanding if you got it,
Otherwise I'll do without it!

When my bones are stiff and aching
And my feet won't climb the stairs,
I will only ask one favor:
Don't bring me no rocking chair.

When you see me walking, stumbling,
Don't study and get it wrong.
'Cause tired don't mean lazy
And every goodbye ain't gone.

I'm the same person I was back then,
A little less hair, a little less chin,
A lot less lungs and much less wind,
But ain't I lucky I can still breathe in.

They went home

They went home and told their wives,
    that never once in all their lives,
    had they known a girl like me,
But…They went home.

They said my house was licking clean,
    no word I spoke was ever mean,
    I had an air of mystery,
But…They went home.

My praises were on all men's lips,
    they liked my smile, my wit, my hips,
    they'd spend one night, or two or three,
But…

Old folks laugh

They have spent their
content of simpering,
holding their lips this
and that way, winding
the lines between
their brows. Old folks
allow their bellies to jiggle like slow
tamborines.
The hollers
rise up and spill
over any way they want.
When old folks laugh, they free the world.
They turn slowly, slyly knowing
the best and worst
of remembering.
Saliva glistens in
the corners of their mouths,
their heads wobble

on brittle necks, but
their laps
are filled with memories.
When old folks laugh, they consider the promise
of dear painless death, and generously
forgive life for happening
to them.

Marjorie Oludhe Macgoye (b 1928)

Macgoye was born in the United Kingdom, and obtained an MA from the
University of London. In 1954 she went to Kenya where she married and became
a Kenyan citizen in 1964 after Independence. She has published three novels,
a collection of poems, a novella and short stories.

A freedom song

Atieno washes dishes,
Atieno plucks the chicken,
Atieno gets up early,
Beds her sacks down in the kitchen,
Atieno eight years old,
Atieno yo.

Since she is my sister's child
Atieno needs no pay,
While she works my wife can sit
Sewing every sunny day:
With her earnings I support
Atieno yo.

Atieno's sly and jealous,
Bad example to the kids
Since she minds them, like a schoolgirl
Wants their dresses, shoes and beads,
Atieno ten years old,
Atieno yo.

Now my wife has gone to study
Atieno is less free.
Don't I keep her, school my own ones,
Pay the party, union fee,

All for progress: aren't you grateful,
Atieno yo?

Visitors need much attention,
All the more when I work night.
That girl spends too long at market,
Who will teach her what is right?
Atieno is rising fourteen,
Atieno yo.

Atieno's had a baby
So we know that she is bad.
Fifty fifty it may live
And repeat the life she had
Ending in post-partum bleeding,
Atieno yo.

Atieno's soon replaced.
Meat and sugar more than all
She ate in such a narrow life
Were lavished on her funeral.
Atieno's gone to glory,
Atieno yo.

Anne Sexton (1928–74)

Sexton was born in Massachusetts, and studied under Robert Lowell (see p. 78) at Boston University, where she later taught. She had been a child model, a member of a jazz band, and a suburban housewife and mother. She suffered a nervous breakdown, was hospitalized, then found some fulfilment in writing. However, when her dependence on alcohol affected her ability to write, she committed suicide at the age of 46.

Compare this poem with Langston Hughes's 'Life is fine' (p. 53).

Wanting to die

Since you ask, most days I cannot remember.
I walk in my clothing, unmarked by that voyage.
Then the almost unnameable lust returns.

Even then I have nothing against life.
I know well the grass blades you mention,
the furniture you have placed under the sun.

But suicides have a special language.
Like carpenters they want to know *which tools.*
They never ask *why build.*

Twice I have so simply declared myself,
have possessed the enemy, eaten the enemy,
have taken on his craft, his magic.

In this way, heavy and thoughtful,
warmer than oil or water,
I have rested, drooling at the mouth-hole.

I did not think of my body at needle point.
Even the cornea and the leftover urine were gone.
Suicides have already betrayed the body.

Still-born, they don't always die,
but dazzled, they can't forget a drug so sweet
that even children would look on and smile.

To thrust all that life under your tongue! –
that, all by itself, becomes a passion.
Death's a sad bone; bruised, you'd say,

and yet she waits for me, year after year,
to so delicately undo an old wound,
to empty my breath from its bad prison.

Balanced there, suicides sometimes meet,
raging at the fruit, a pumped-up moon,
leaving the bread they mistook for a kiss,

leaving the page of the book carelessly open,
something unsaid, the phone off the hook
and the love, whatever it was, an infection.

U A (Ursula Askham) Fanthorpe (b 1929)

Fanthorpe was born in London and studied at Oxford. She has taught English
at a number of schools and universities. Six collections of her poems have been
published.

You will be hearing from us shortly

You feel adequate to the demands of this position?
What qualities do you feel you
Personally have to offer?

                                                    Ah

Let us consider your application form.
Your qualifications, though impressive, are
Not, we must admit, precisely what
We had in mind. Would you care
To defend their relevance?

                                                Indeed

Now your age. Perhaps you feel able
To make your own comment about that,
Too? We are conscious ourselves
Of the need for a candidate with precisely
The right degree of immaturity.

                                    So glad we agree

And now a delicate matter: your looks.
You do appreciate this work involves
Contact with the actual public? Might they,
Perhaps, find your appearance
Disturbing?

                                              Quite so

And your accent. That is the way
You have always spoken, is it? What
Of your education? Were
You educated? We mean, of course,
Where were you educated?
                              And how
Much of a handicap is that to you,
Would you say?

                    Married, children,
We see. The usual dubious
Desire to perpetuate what had better
Not have happened at all. We do not
Ask what domestic disasters shimmer
Behind that vaguely unsuitable address.

And you were born –?

                                        Yes. Pity

So glad we agree.

Thom Gunn (b 1929)

Gunn was born in the United Kingdom. Shortly after the appearance of his first book of poems *Fighting Terms* he went to teach at Stanford University in the United States, and in 1960 settled permanently in San Francisco.

On the move

'Man, you gotta Go.'

The blue jay scuffling in the bushes follows
Some hidden purpose, and the gust of birds
That spurts across the field, the wheeling swallows,
Have nested in the trees and undergrowth.
Seeking their instinct, or their poise, or both,
One moves with an uncertain violence
Under the dust thrown by a baffled sense
Or the dull thunder of approximate words.

On motorcycles, up the road, they come:
Small, black, as flies hanging in heat, the Boys,
Until the distance throws them forth, their hum
Bulges to thunder held by calf and thigh.
In goggles, donned impersonality,
In gleaming jackets trophied with the dust,
They strap in doubt – by hiding it, robust –
And almost hear a meaning in their noise.

Exact conclusion of their hardiness
Has no shape yet, but from known whereabouts
They ride, direction where the tires press.
They scare a flight of birds across the field:
Much that is natural, to the will must yield.
Men manufacture both machine and soul,
And use what they imperfectly control
To dare a future from the taken routes.

It is part solution, after all.
One is not necessarily discord
On earth; or damned because, half animal,

One lacks direct instinct, because one wakes
Afloat on movement that divides and breaks.
One joins the movement in a valueless world,
Choosing it, till, both hurler and the hurled,
One moves as well, always toward, toward.

A minute holds them, who have come to go:
The self-defined, astride the created will
They burst away; the towns they travel through
Are home for neither bird nor holiness,
For birds and saints complete their purposes.
At worst, one is in motion; and at best,
Reaching no absolute, in which to rest,
One is always nearer by not keeping still.

James Matthews (b 1929)

Matthews was born in Athlone near Cape Town. He has published four
collections of his poems, and a book of short stories. He founded Blac
Publishing House.

For the word 'pass' in this poem, see the note that precedes Mafika Pascal
Gwala's poem 'Kwela-ride' (p. 192).

the face of my mother takes the shape

the face of my mother takes the shape of
a frightened mouse
at the sound of a policeman's step
the fear-filled flutter of her heart
a bird ensnared
my father freezes his feelings at the demand
for a pass
and i watch the fire in his
eyes slowly die
as his hands grope for the right to survive

Adrienne Rich (b 1929)

Rich was born in Baltimore in the United States. Since the selection of her first
volume by W H Auden for the Yale series of Younger Poets in 1951, her work has
continually broken new ground.

Song

You're wondering if I'm lonely:
OK then, yes, I'm lonely
as a plane rides lonely and level
on its radio beam, aiming
across the Rockies
for the blue-strung aisles
of an airfield on the ocean

You want to ask, am I lonely?
Well, of course, lonely
as a woman driving across country
day after day, leaving behind
mile after mile
little towns she might have stopped
and lived and died in, lonely

If I'm lonely
it must be the loneliness
of waking first, of breathing
dawn's first cold breath on the city
of being the one awake
in a house wrapped in sleep

If I'm lonely
it's with the rowboat ice-fast on the shore
in the last red light of the year
that knows what it is, that knows it's neither
ice nor mud nor winter light
but wood, with a gift for burning

Helen Segal (1929 – 88)

Segal was born in Johannesburg, and earned degrees from the University of the
Witwatersrand and Unisa. She worked as a teacher and as an office-worker. Her
only collection of poems *Lacking a Label* was published in 1974.

Let's do away with the show

Let's do away
with the show –
the smart slick
spectacle
of the
twentieth-century
living room

cultivate
a little shyness
and a little dust –

the shabbiness
of well-used
chairs
that understand
anatomy

face each other
if we can

Chinua Achebe (b 1930)

Achebe was born in Nigeria. He is best known as a novelist: *Things Fall Apart, No Longer At Ease, Arrow of God, A Man of the People, Anthills of the Savannah.* He supported the Biafrans during the Nigerian civil war. His single collection of poems is *Beware, Soul Brother*. He could be said to be the most influential and respected African writer in English.

Refugee mother and child

No Madonna and Child could touch
that picture of a mother's tenderness
for a son she soon would have to forget.

The air was heavy with odours
of diarrhoea of unwashed children
with washed-out ribs and dried-up
bottoms struggling in laboured
steps behind blown empty bellies. Most
mothers there had long ceased

to care but not this one; she held
a ghost smile between her teeth
and in her eyes the ghost of a mother's
pride as she combed the rust-coloured
hair left on his skull and then –
singing in her eyes – began carefully
to part it … In another life this
would have been a little daily
act of no consequence before his
breakfast and school; now she
did it like putting flowers
on a tiny grave.

Chinua Achebe gives this note to the following poem: 'Many years ago a strange and terrible thing happened in the small village of Ogbaku. A lawyer driving through the highway that passes by that village ran over a man. The villagers, thinking the man was killed, set upon the lawyer and clubbed him to death. Then to their horror, their man began to stir. So, the story went, they set upon him too and finished him off, saying, "You can't come back having made us do that."'

Lazarus

We know the breath-taking
joy of his sisters when the word
spread: He is risen! But a
man who has lived a full life
will have others to
reckon with beside his
sisters. Certainly that keen-eyed
subordinate who has moved up
to his table at the office, for
him resurrection is an awful
embarrassment … The luckless
people of Ogbaku knew its
terrors that day the twin-headed
evil strode their highway. It
could not have been easy
picking up again the blood-spattered
clubs they had cast away; or to
turn from the battered body
of the barrister lying beside his
battered limousine to finish off

their own man, stirring now suddenly
in wide-eyed resurrection … How well
they understood those grim-faced
villagers wielding their crimson
weapons once more that at the hour
of his rising their kinsman
avenged in murder would turn
away from them in obedience
to other fraternities, would turn indeed
their own accuser and in one
breath obliterate their plea
and justification! So they killed
him a second time that day on the
threshold of a promising resurrection.

Ted Hughes (b 1930)

Hughes was born in the United Kingdom. He studied at Cambridge University, and at the age of 26 married the American poet Sylvia Plath (see p. 138). In 1963 she committed suicide, leaving two small children. In 1969 his partner Assia Wevill committed suicide in exactly the same way, also taking the life of their daughter. Hughes married again in 1970. In 1984 Hughes was appointed Poet Laureate of the United Kingdom (which means he is required to write poems for state occasions).

This next poem is about writing a poem; is it also about seeing a fox at night?

The thought-fox

I imagine this midnight moment's forest:
Something else is alive
Beside the clock's loneliness
And this blank page where my fingers move.

Through the window I see no star:
Something more near
Though deeper within darkness
Is entering the loneliness:

Cold, delicately as the dark snow
A fox's nose touches twig, leaf;
Two eyes serve a movement, that now
And again now, and now, and now

Sets neat prints into the snow
Between trees, and warily a lame
Shadow lags by stump and in hollow
Of a body that is bold to come

Across clearings, an eye,
A widening deepening greenness,
Brilliantly, concentratedly,
Coming about its own business

Till, with a sudden sharp hot stink of fox
It enters the dark hole of the head.
The window is starless still; the clock ticks,
The page is printed.

Hughes does not say, but one wonders if what follows is a posthumous portrait of his first wife, the poet Sylvia Plath (see p. 138). See also the Chaucer extracts on p. 1.

Chaucer

'Whan that Aprille with his shoures soote
The droghte of March hath perced to the roote ...'
At the top of your voice, where you swayed on the top of a stile,
Your arms raised – somewhat for balance, somewhat
To hold the reins of the straining attention
Of your imagined audience – you declaimed Chaucer
To a field of cows. And the Spring sky had done it
With its flying laundry, and the new emerald
Of the thorns, the hawthorn, the blackthorn,
And one of those bumpers of champagne
You snatched unpredictably from pure spirit.
Your voice went over the fields towards Grantchester.
It must have sounded lost. But the cows
Watched, then approached: they appreciated Chaucer.
You went on and on. Here were reasons
To recite Chaucer. Then came the Wyf of Bath,
Your favourite character in all literature.
You were rapt. And the cows were enthralled.
They shoved and jostled shoulders, making a ring,
To gaze into your face, with occasional snorts
Of exclamation, renewed their astounded attention,

Ears angling to catch every inflection,
Keeping their awed six feet of reverence
Away from you. You just could not believe it.
And you could not stop. What would happen
If you were to stop? Would they attack you,
Scared by the shock of silence, or wanting more –?
So you had to go on. You went on –
And twenty cows stayed with you hypnotized.
How did you stop? I can't remember
You stopping. I imagine they reeled away –
Rolling eyes, as if driven from their fodder.
I imagine I shooed them away. But
Your sostenuto rendering of Chaucer
Was already perpetual. What followed
Found my attention too full
And had to go back into oblivion.

Mazisi Kunene (b 1930)

Kunene was born in Durban. From the University of Natal he obtained a
BA Honours, an MA and a Doctorate in Literature. He taught at the National
University of Lesotho, and in 1959 went into exile and was one of the founders
of the Anti-Apartheid Movement. He has taught at a number of American
universities, and is a world authority on Zulu poetry and literature.

When you have read the next poem, see also Fhazel Johennesse's 'a young
man's thoughts before june the 16th' (p. 237), Don Mattera's 'Let the children
decide' (p. 153), and Donald Parenzee's 'Then the children decided' (p. 202).

Congregation of the story-tellers
at a funeral of Soweto children

We have entered the night to tell our tale,
To listen to those who have not spoken.
We, who have seen our children die in the morning,
Deserve to be listened to.
We have looked on blankly as they opened their wounds.
Nothing really matters except the grief of our children.
Their tears must be revered,
Their inner silence speaks louder than the spoken word;
And all being and all life shouts out in outrage.
We must not be rushed to our truths.

Whatever we failed to say is stored secretly in our minds;
And all those processions of embittered crowds
Have seen us lead them a thousand times.
We can hear the story over and over again,
Our minds are numbed beyond the sadness,
We have received the power to command;
There is nothing more we can fear.

Marie Philip (b 1930)

Philip lives in Cape Town, where she was born. She has spent much of her
working life in publishing. She and her husband David became independent
publishers in 1971.

Black dog

One has been
everybody else's property
for weeks –
they know about weddings.
Every detail – 'tea for the traffic cop' –
has been meticulously planned,
and the family now is rising through the organization
to the occasion: the date and almost the time.

A deluge of Autumn rain gives my father the opportunity
of reminding no one
that he refused to have a garden reception
and multiple anxieties are locked away
in his tower of strength.
I too have been charming all day.
Veiled now, and dispensing white serenity,
I wave off ahead of me
my mother and my festooned retinue
and accept my father's arm
past puddles
to the hired and chauffeured car.

Sharp barks. A muddy Scotch terrier
hurtles himself on this dressed-up neighbour
and I screech:
'Buggeroff you-bloody-little-black-dog.'

Remorse! Image sullied, I turn to my father,
and face a rare enjoyment, feel a tightened arm.
From a clean moment of contact
we proceed with ceremony
for him formally
to give me away.

Derek Walcott (b 1930)

Walcott was born in Trinidad and is the best-known West Indian poet and
playwright. In 1988 he received the Queen's Gold Medal for Poetry; in 1991 he
won the W H Smith Literary Award; and in 1992 he was awarded the Nobel Prize
for Literature.

Compare this West Indian poem with the two South African poems that have
the title 'Mantis', by Robert Dederick (p. 80) and Ruth Miller (p. 82).

From *A tropical bestiary*
Lizard

Fear:
        the heraldic lizard, magnified,
Devouring its midge.
                Last night I plucked
'as a brand from the burning', a murderous, pincered beetle
Floundering in urine like a shipwreck shallop
Rudderless, its legs frantic as oars.
Did I, by this act, set things right side up?
It was not death I dreaded but the fight
With nothing. The aged, flailing their claws
On flowery coverlets, may dread such salvation,
The impotence of rescue or compassion.
Rightening a beetle damns creation.
It may have felt more terror on its back
When my delivering fingers, huge as hell,
Shadowed the stiffening victim with their jaws
Than the brown lizard, Galapagos-large,
Waggling its horny tail at morning's morsel
Held for the midge.
                Mercy has strange laws.
Withdraw and leave the scheme of things in charge.

The fist

The fist clenched round my heart
loosens a little, and I gasp
brightness; but it tightens
again. When have I ever not loved
the pain of love? But this has moved

past love to mania. This has the strong
clench of the madman, this is
gripping the ledge of unreason, before
plunging howling into the abyss.

Hold hard then, heart. This way at least you live.

Stan Motjuwadi (1931–90)

Motjuwadi was one of the famous *Drum* magazine writers in the 1950s.
In the 1970s and 1980s he returned to the magazine and was its editor for
a number of years.
See the note preceding Mafika Gwala's poem 'Kwela-ride' (p. 192).

Taken for a ride

I get my cue
from the glint in the cop's eye.
I have seen it before.
So I have to find it.

I pull away from Mono
and hug myself in desperation.
Up, down, back, front, sides,
like a crazed tribal dancer.
I have to find it.

Without it I'm lost, with it I'm lost,
a cipher in Albert Street.
I hate it. I nurse it,
my pass, my everything.

Up, down, back, front, sides,
Mono's lip twitches,
She looks at me with all the love.

She shakes her head nervously.
Up, front, sides, back, down,
like a crazed tribal dancer.
Molimo!

The doors of the kwela-kwela gape,
I jabber at Mono.
The doors swing lazy, sadistic like Jonah's whale.
I take a free ride.

Patrick Cullinan (b 1932)

Cullinan was born in Pretoria, studied at Oxford, has been a saw-miller in
Machadodorp, has run a publishing house, and has taught at the University
of the Western Cape. Four collections of poems were followed by his *Selected
Poems* in 1995.

The beach, the evening

And now the tide's way out, the sun just hot
And a wide buck nigger in blue jeans walks
The open sand. The whites glare. Black. It's not
Just colour it's his stance. He preens, he stalks.

All his body swings with nerve, with pounds
Of insolence. Slap into the waves
He bounces fully clad. And this astounds
No one. He leaps and waves his arms. He saves

Nothing. Emerges dripping, shining. Rapist!
Faker! Hopped up, slapping wet, he doubles
On the spot: then does a backward twist.
An exercise that no one sees, troubles

To see. He lopes off. Disappears. And on
The pink horizon a yacht comes up, met
By stares and tea time. All day has gone.
And now: red sails. The bloody sunset.

The first, far beat

In the mountains
the first, far beat
of spring thunder:

thick with young,
a lizard on the rock
moves its head

and in the flank
the quick heart pulses.

Jenny Joseph (b 1932)

Joseph was born in Birmingham in the United Kingdom. She studied at
Oxford University, and has had a considerable number of collections of poems
published. She has worked as a newspaper reporter, an adult education lecturer,
and a pub landlady, and has lived in South Africa. This is the one poem of hers
that is most frequently anthologized.

Warning

When I am an old woman I shall wear purple
With a red hat which doesn't go, and doesn't suit me,
And I shall spend my pension on brandy and summer gloves
And satin sandals, and say we've no money for butter.
I shall sit down on the pavement when I'm tired
And gobble up samples in shops and press alarm bells
And run my stick along the public railings
And make up for the sobriety of my youth.
I shall go out in my slippers in the rain
And pick the flowers in other people's gardens
And learn to spit.

You can wear terrible shirts and grow more fat
And eat three pounds of sausages at a go
Or only bread and pickle for a week
And hoard pens and pencils and beermats and things in boxes.

But now we must have clothes that keep us dry
And pay our rent and not swear in the street

And set a good example for the children.
We will have friends to dinner and read the papers.

But maybe I ought to practise a little now?
So people who know me are not too shocked and surprised
When suddenly I am old and start to wear purple.

Douglas Livingstone (1932–96)

Livingstone was born in Kuala Lumpur in Malaysia. His family moved to
what was then Natal, where he had his school education. He qualified as a
bacteriologist and worked in Zimbabwe and Zambia, before taking up a post
in marine biology in Durban. An internationally-known poet, he had nine
volumes of poetry published, his *Selected Poems* winning the CNA Literary
Award in 1985.

Blue stuff

Wall-to-wall city on a rainy night; eleven
stories up and the wonder-hour-hand when
is 4 a.m. with only a very quiet Kenton
accompanying the one-sky-lamp in

the corner. Yes, she's gone, warm to bed.
The floor feels strangely concrete-solid
despite the undermining gusts walled outside.
Wet beetles lie parked under street lamps, dead.

The wakeful rain musics back no April
in Paris; nor stale old Stars fell
on Alabama. Somewhere, space unfurls
its furnaced seasons. Somewhere, over the sill,

crooked as the iced-sucker wrapper flies,
the holiday surf, swelled into its own, says:
The sshun'sh gone. The night-tide ebbs and soughs
loud and lording it unchallenged upon the shores

of South Beach, North Beach, Country Club.
Even the sherry-drinkers have long stubbed
the last drag. The street's hands are cupped;
the stars, maybe forever, are all washed up.

Gentling a wildcat

Not much wild life, roared Mine leonine Host
from the fringe of a forest of crackles
round an old dome-headed steam radio,
between hotel and river – a mile of bush –
except for the wildcats and jackals.

And he, of these parts for years, was right.
That evening I ventured with no trepidations
and a torch, towed by the faculty
I cannot understand, that has got me
into too many situations.

Under a tree, in filtered moonlight,
a ragged heap of dusty leaves stopped moving.
A cat lay there, open from chin to loins;
lower viscera missing; truncated tubes
and bitten-off things protruding.

Little blood there was, but a mess of
damaged lungs; straining to hold its breath
for quiet; claws fixed curved and jutting,
jammed open in a stench of jackal meat;
it tried to raise its head hating the mystery, death.

The big spade-skull with its lynx-fat cheeks
aggressive still, raging eyes hooked in me, game;
nostrils pulling at a tight mask of anger
and fear; then I remembered hearing
they are quite impossible to tame.

Closely, in a bowl of unmoving roots,
an untouched carcass, unlicked, swaddled and wrapped
in trappings of birth, the first of a litter stretched.
Rooted out in mid-confinement: a time
when jackals have courage enough for a wildcat.

In some things, too, I am a coward,
and could not here punch down with braced thumb,
lift the nullifying stone or stiff-edged hand
to axe with mercy the nape of her spine.
Besides, I convinced myself, she was numb.

And oppressively, something felt wrong:
not her approaching melting with earth,
but in lifetimes of claws, kaleidoscopes:
moon-claws, sun-claws, teeth after death,
certainly both at mating and birth.

So I sat and gentled her with my hand,
not moving much but saying things, using my voice;
and she became gentle, affording herself
the influent luxury of breathing –
untrammelled, bubbly, safe in its noise.

Later, calmed, despite her tides of pain,
she let me ease her claws, the ends of the battle,
pulling off the trapped and rancid flesh.
Her miniature limbs of iron relaxed.
She died with hardly a rattle.

I placed her peaceful ungrinning corpse
and that of her firstborn in the topgallants
of a young tree, out of ground reach, to grow: restart
a cycle of maybe something more pastoral
commencing with beetles, then maggots, then ants.

The 'Station 19' referred to in the next poem is a sampling station around
Durban where much of Livingstone's work as a marine bacteriologist took place.

Scourings at Station 19

After the floods, debris heaped higher than two men
spreads wider than two dozen. Pistoned out to sea
by rain-rammed waterways: whole swathes of riverbank,
shreds of homemade dwellings, furniture, sheets of tin,
corners of concrete, trees, reeds fuse with sugar-cane.

Donkey carcasses, cows, stiff-legged bushbuck distend
among half-dead disoriented hair-triggered snakes.
Bad for the tourists. The whole infected mish-mash
rejected by the waves, beached now, starting to rot,
choking the coast for leagues, waits on the bulldozers.

On one high peak, (a pain for the SPCA
if ever there was one!) a roughed up bantam stands
still handsome if glazed, his feathers skew; orange, brown,
scarlet and black dusty with sand and wrung out brine
– no steepled vane yawing above ordered pews here.

Drowning out the now docile surf, yellow eye fierce,
he bellows his polysyllabic epithet
at the horizon where the crouched sun hesitates
on the threshold of all that vehemence: too much
inexorability for a straight All Clear.

This teapot, whose rage is writ too large to be cooped
within one pygmy chanticleer, surveyed amazed
by gulls and gannets, trumpets his fractious challenge.
Tempting to dub the din thanksgiving; or more: life
triumphs even on no longer trusted planets.

Christopher Okigbo (1932–67)

Okigbo was born in the small village of Ojoto in the Eastern Region of Nigeria,
into an Igbo family. After his university education in Ibadan, when the Nigerian
civil war broke out he joined other Igbos in moving to the newly-formed state of
Biafra. He enlisted in the Biafran army, but, three months later at the age of 35,
he was killed in action. By then he had achieved a reputation as Nigeria's
foremost poet.

The complex poem that follows is part of a sequence with the title 'Path
of Thunder: Poems Prophesying War'. You might like to consider Okigbo's
disarming comment: 'If the poem can elicit a response in either physical or
emotional terms...the poem has succeeded. I don't think I have ever set out to
communicate a meaning.' There are a number of glancing allusions in the poem:
for instance, to C P Snow's then recently-published novel *Corridors of Power*,
Chinua Achebe's novel *Arrow of God*, Cyprian Ekwensi's *Brush Fire,* and August
Strindberg's play *Dance of Death*.

Come thunder

Now that the triumphant march has entered the last street corners,
Remember, O dancers, the thunder among the clouds...

Now that laughter, broken in two, hangs tremulous between the teeth,
Remember, O dancers, the lightning beyond the earth...

The smell of blood already floats in the lavender-mist of the afternoon.
The death sentence lies in ambush along the corridors of power;
And a great fearful thing already tugs at the cables of the open air,
A nebula immense and immeasurable, a night of deep waters –
An iron dream unnamed and unprintable, a path of stone.

The drowsy heads of the pods in barren farmlands witness it,
The homesteads abandoned in this century's brush fire witness it:
The myriad eyes of deserted corn cobs in burning barns witness it:
Magic birds with the miracle of lightning flash on their feathers ...

The arrows of God tremble at the gates of light,
The drums of curfew pander to a dance of death;

And the secret thing in its heaving
Threatens with iron mask
The last lighted torch of the century ...

Lenrie Peters (b 1932)

Peters was born in The Gambia. He studied medicine in Freetown in Sierra
Leone and then at Trinity College, Cambridge. He practises as a surgeon.

Parachute men say

Parachute men say
The first jump
Takes the breath away
Feet in the air disturb
Till you get used to it.

Solid ground
Is not where you left it
As you plunge down
Perhaps head first
As you listen to
Your arteries talking
You learn to sustain hope.

Suddenly you are only
Holding an umbrella
In a windy place
As the warm earth

Reaches out to you
Reassures you
The vibrating interim is over.

You try to land
Where green grass yields
And carry your pack
Across the fields

The violent arrival
Puts out the joint
Earth has nowhere to go
You are at the starting point

Jumping across worlds
In condensed time
After the awkward fall
We are always at the starting point

Sylvia Plath (1932–63)

Plath was born in the United States of America. She followed a brilliant student career at Smith College with a scholarship to Cambridge University. There she met the young poet Ted Hughes (see p. 125); within four months they were married. After the birth of their second child, they separated and, some months later, Sylvia Plath committed suicide by putting her head into a gas oven (she had attempted suicide before, in America at the age of 20). She had written an autobiographical novel *The Bell Jar* and, shortly before her death, she wrote the extremely powerful poems on which her reputation largely rests, published after her death under the title *Ariel*. Hughes has since edited her *Collected Poems* and her *Journals*, while her mother has edited her *Letters Home*.

Frieda, the daughter of Sylvia Plath and Ted Hughes, was conceived while they were in America in the middle of 1959 and was born on 1 April 1960 in the United Kingdom. This poem was written in January–February 1960 to the unborn child. See also Grace Nichols's poem 'In my name' (p. 220).

You're

Clownlike, happiest on your hands,
Feet to the stars, and moon-skulled,
Gilled like a fish. A common-sense
Thumbs-down on the dodo's mode.
Wrapped up in yourself like a spool,

Trawling your dark as owls do.
Mute as a turnip from the Fourth
Of July to All Fools' Day,
O high-riser, my little loaf.

Vague as fog and looked for like mail.
Farther off than Australia.
Bent-backed Atlas, our traveled prawn.
Snug as a bud and at home
Like a sprat in a pickle jug.
A creel of eels, all ripples.
Jumpy as a Mexican bean.
Right, like a well-done sum.
A clean slate, with your own face on.

Sylvia Plath's father, an entomologist, had been a beekeeper, and had written
a book about bees. When she and Ted Hughes bought a house in Devon, she
joined a beekeeping society and briefly kept one hive. The next poem, and four
other 'bee poems', were written within the same week in October 1962. In
another of the bee poems she describes the protective clothing the beekeepers
wear: gloves, long smocks, hats with veils attached to them.

The arrival of the bee box

I ordered this, this clean wood box
Square as a chair and almost too heavy to lift.
I would say it was the coffin of a midget
Or a square baby
Were there not such a din in it.

The box is locked, it is dangerous.
I have to live with it overnight
And I can't keep away from it.
There are no windows, so I can't see what is in there.
There is only a little grid, no exit.

I put my eye to the grid.
It is dark, dark,
With the swarmy feeling of African hands
Minute and shrunk for export,
Black on black, angrily clambering.

How can I let them out?
It is the noise that appalls me most of all,
The unintelligible syllables.
It is like a Roman mob,
Small, taken one by one, but my god, together!

I lay my ear to furious Latin.
I am not a Caesar.
I have simply ordered a box of maniacs.
They can be sent back.
They can die, I need feed them nothing, I am the owner.

I wonder how hungry they are.
I wonder if they would forget me
If I just undid the locks and stood back and turned into a tree.
There is the laburnum, its blond colonnades,
And the petticoats of the cherry.

They might ignore me immediately
In my moon suit and funeral veil.
I am no source of honey
So why should they turn on me?
Tomorrow I will be sweet God, I will set them free.

The box is only temporary.

The following poem was written while Sylvia Plath was in hospital for an
appendectomy in 1961.

Tulips

The tulips are too excitable, it is winter here.
Look how white everything is, how quiet, how snowed-in.
I am learning peacefulness, lying by myself quietly
As the light lies on these white walls, this bed, these hands.
I am nobody; I have nothing to do with explosions.
I have given my name and my day-clothes up to the nurses
And my history to the anesthetist and my body to surgeons.

They have propped my head between the pillow and the sheet-cuff
Like an eye between two white lids that will not shut.
Stupid pupil, it has to take everything in.
The nurses pass and pass, they are no trouble,

They pass the way gulls pass inland in their white caps,
Doing things with their hands, one just the same as another,
So it is impossible to tell how many there are.

My body is a pebble to them, they tend it as water
Tends to the pebbles it must run over, smoothing them gently.
They bring me numbness in their bright needles, they bring me sleep.
Now I have lost myself I am sick of baggage –
My patent leather overnight case like a black pillbox,
My husband and child smiling out of the family photo;
Their smiles catch onto my skin, little smiling hooks.

I have let things slip, a thirty-year-old cargo boat
Stubbornly hanging on to my name and address.
They have swabbed me clear of my loving associations.
Scared and bare on the green plastic-pillowed trolley
I watched my teaset, my bureaus of linen, my books
Sink out of sight, and the water went over my head.
I am a nun now, I have never been so pure.

I didn't want any flowers, I only wanted
To lie with my hands turned up and be utterly empty.
How free it is, you have no idea how free –
The peacefulness is so big it dazes you,
And it asks nothing, a name tag, a few trinkets.
It is what the dead close on, finally; I imagine them
Shutting their mouths on it, like a Communion tablet.

The tulips are too red in the first place, they hurt me.
Even through the gift paper I could hear them breathe
Lightly, through their white swaddlings, like an awful baby.
Their redness talks to my wound, it corresponds.
They are subtle: they seem to float, though they weigh me down,
Upsetting me with their sudden tongues and their color,
A dozen red lead sinkers round my neck.

Nobody watched me before, now I am watched.
The tulips turn to me, and the window behind me
Where once a day the light slowly widens and slowly thins,
And I see myself, flat, ridiculous, a cut-paper shadow
Between the eye of the sun and the eyes of the tulips,
And I have no face, I have wanted to efface myself.
The vivid tulips eat my oxygen.

Before they came the air was calm enough,
Coming and going, breath by breath, without any fuss.
Then the tulips filled it up like a loud noise.
Now the air snags and eddies round them the way a river
Snags and eddies round a sunken rust-red engine.
They concentrate my attention, that was happy
Playing and resting without committing itself.

The walls, also, seem to be warming themselves.
The tulips should be behind bars like dangerous animals;
They are opening like the mouth of some great African cat,
And I am aware of my heart: it opens and closes
Its bowl of red blooms out of sheer love of me.
The water I taste is warm and salt, like the sea,
And comes from a country far away as health.

Sylvia Plath's father was German, and died when she was eight years old. This poem, written when she was 30, shows how important he was to her. He was not, of course, a Nazi. In addition to her father, the poem concerns the second father-figure in her life, her husband Ted Hughes. By the time she wrote the poem they were already separated.

Daddy

You do not do, you do not do
Any more, black shoe
In which I have lived like a foot
For thirty years, poor and white,
Barely daring to breathe or Achoo.

Daddy, I have had to kill you.
You died before I had time –
Marble-heavy, a bag full of God,
Ghastly statue with one gray toe
Big as a Frisco seal

And a head in the freakish Atlantic
Where it pours bean green over blue
In the waters off beautiful Nauset.
I used to pray to recover you.
Ach, du.

In the German tongue, in the Polish town
Scraped flat by the roller
Of wars, wars, wars.
But the name of the town is common.
My Polack friend

Says there are a dozen or two.
So I never could tell where you
Put your foot, your root,
I never could talk to you.
The tongue stuck in my jaw.

It stuck in a barb wire snare.
Ich, ich, ich, ich,
I could hardly speak.
I thought every German was you.
And the language obscene

An engine, an engine
Chuffing me off like a Jew.
A Jew to Dachau, Auschwitz, Belsen.
I began to talk like a Jew.
I think I may well be a Jew.

The snows of the Tyrol, the clear beer of Vienna
Are not very pure or true.
With my gipsy ancestress and my weird luck
And my Taroc pack and my Taroc pack
I may be a bit of a Jew.

I have always been scared of *you*,
With your Luftwaffe, your gobbledygoo.
And your neat mustache
And your Aryan eye, bright blue.
Panzer-man, panzer-man, O You –

Not God but a swastika
So black no sky could squeak through.
Every woman adores a Fascist,
The boot in the face, the brute
Brute heart of a brute like you.

You stand at the blackboard, daddy,
In the picture I have of you,
A cleft in your chin instead of your foot
But no less a devil for that, no not
Any less the black man who

Bit my pretty red heart in two.
I was ten when they buried you.
At twenty I tried to die
And get back, back, back to you.
I thought even the bones would do.

But they pulled me out of the sack,
And they stuck me together with glue.
And then I knew what to do.
I made a model of you,
A man in black with a Meinkampf look

And a love of the rack and the screw.
And I said I do, I do.
So daddy, I'm finally through.
The black telephone's off at the root,
The voices just can't worm through.

If I've killed one man, I've killed two –
The vampire who said he was you
And drank my blood for a year,
Seven years, if you want to know.
Daddy, you can lie back now.

There's a stake in your fat black heart
And the villagers never liked you.
They are dancing and stamping on you.
They always *knew* it was you.
Daddy, daddy, you bastard, I'm through.

Anne Stevenson (b 1933)

Stevenson was born in the United Kingdom, brought up in the United States, educated at the University of Michigan, and now lives in the United Kingdom. She is well known for her biography of the poet Sylvia Plath (see p. 138), called *Bitter Fame*.

The victory

I thought you were my victory
though you cut me like a knife
when I brought you out of my body
into your life.

Tiny antagonist, gory,
blue as a bruise. The stains
of your cloud of glory
bled from my veins.

How can you dare, blind thing,
blank insect eyes?
You barb the air. You sting
with bladed cries.

Snail!   Scary knot of desires!
Hungry snarl!   Small son.
Why do I have to love you?
How have you won?

Utah

Somewhere nowhere in Utah, a boy by the roadside,
gun in his hand, and the rare dumb hard tears flowing.
Beside him, the greyheaded man has let one arm slide
awkwardly over his shoulder, is talking and pointing
at whatever it is, dead, in the dust on the ground.

By the old parked Chevy, two women, talking and watching.
Their skirts flag forward. Bandannas twist with their hair.
Around them some sheep and a fence and the sagebrush burning
and burning with its blue flame. In the distance, where
the mountains are clouds, lightning, but no rain.

Wole Soyinka (b 1934)

Soyinka was born in Nigeria. He studied at the Universities of Ibadan in Nigeria and Leeds in the United Kingdom; he also worked at the Royal Court Theatre in London. It is during this period that 'Telephone conversation' was written. In 1960 he returned to Nigeria to teach at the University of Ibadan. In 1967 at the start of the Nigerian civil war he was arrested and imprisoned (apparently for his support of Biafra, though he was never charged). Twenty-seven months later he was released. In 1986 he was awarded the Nobel Prize for Literature. In 1994 his passport was withdrawn by the Nigerian military government and he escaped into exile in Europe.

Telephone conversation

The price seemed reasonable, location
Indifferent. The landlady swore she lived
Off premises. Nothing remained
But self-confession. 'Madam,' I warned,
'I hate a wasted journey – I am African.'
Silence. Silenced transmission of
Pressurized good-breeding. Voice, when it came,
Lipstick coated, long gold-rolled
Cigarette-holder pipped. Caught I was, foully.
'HOW DARK?' … I had not misheard … 'ARE YOU LIGHT
OR VERY DARK?' Button B. Button A. Stench
Of rancid breath of public hide-and-speak.
Red booth. Red pillar-box. Red double-tiered
Omnibus squelching tar. It *was* real! Shamed
By ill-mannered silence, surrender
Pushed dumbfoundment to beg simplification.
Considerate she was, varying the emphasis –
'ARE YOU DARK? OR VERY LIGHT?' Revelation came.
'You mean – like plain or milk chocolate?'
Her assent was clinical, crushing in its light
Impersonality. Rapidly, wave-length adjusted,
I chose. 'West African sepia' – and as afterthought,
'Down in my passport.' Silence for spectroscopic
Flight of fancy, till truthfulness clanged her accent
Hard on the mouthpiece. 'WHAT'S THAT?' conceding
'DON'T KNOW WHAT THAT IS.' 'Like brunette.'
'THAT'S DARK, ISN'T IT?' 'Not altogether.
Facially, I am brunette, but madam, you should see

The rest of me. Palm of my hand, soles of my feet
Are a peroxide blonde. Friction, caused –
Foolishly madam – by sitting down, has turned
My bottom raven black – One moment madam!' – sensing
Her receiver rearing on the thunderclap
About my ears – 'Madam,' I pleaded, 'wouldn't you rather
See for yourself?'

The next poem was written while Soyinka was in solitary confinement in prison, 1967–69.

To the madmen over the wall

Howl, howl
Your fill and overripeness of the heart,
I may not come with you
Companions of the broken buoy
I may not seek
The harbour of your drifting shore.

Your wise withdrawal
Who can blame? Crouched
Upon your ledge of space, do you witness
Ashes of reality drift strangely past?
I fear
Your minds have dared the infinite
And journeyed back
To speak in foreign tongues.

Though walls
May rupture tired seams
Of the magic cloak we share, yet
Closer I may not come
But though I set my ears against
The tune of setting forth, yet, howl
Upon the hour of sleep, tell these walls
The human heart may hold
Only so much despair.

Zulfikar Ghose (b 1935)

Ghose was born in Sialkot in what became Pakistan. His family moved to the
United Kingdom in 1952. He completed his education at Keele University, and
became a cricket and hockey correspondent for the *Observer* newspaper. In 1969
he moved to the University of Texas. Regarded as Pakistan's major poet, he has
published a number of collections, as well as novels and autobiographical
works.

India became independent of Britain in August 1947; the subcontinent
was divided into India and Pakistan. Mahatma Gandhi was assassinated on
30 January 1948. The poet gives this note to the poem: 'Gandhi was assassinated
when he was coming to his prayer meeting, not during it as Part II of this poem
might suggest.'

The loss of India

I

Eagles cartwheeled above the illuminations
of Independence Day, the dogs sniffed at
the electric bulbs which sizzled like fat.

The tall grass the monsoons left on the mountains
was aflame like corn in the setting August sun.
Two stones collided, sparked. India began to burn.

II

At Mahatma Gandhi's prayer meeting,
under Asoka's wheel on the tricolour,
the air intoning religious verses,
a man stood in the scabbard of the crowd,
a machine gun at the tip of his zealous tongue.
What well-tutored doves the politicians
had released into the skies above Delhi
had already blackened with the soot
of communal hatred. The air chanted
the Bhagvat Gita, the Koran and the Bible.
Gandhi nodded, warmed by his goat's-milk diet,
a Moses and a Mohammed thinned
to the bones of a self-denying innocence,
mild as foam on the tortured crest of his
people's violence, straight as a walking stick
on the savage contours of his country.

When the bullets hit him, his body was cut
into the bars of a jail he had never left,
his stomach shrivelled in another hunger fast.

III

A boy in the street, sulking in his boots,
kicked at stones and pouted his lips at crows.
There was the shade to retreat to, the doors

to be behind. But the pride of mountains
annoyed him, the neighing peaks loud
with thunder exhaling the smoke of monsoon clouds.

His nostrils twitched like a cow's when a fly
sits there. For the sea air of Bombay was
salt, dry. And how could he describe his loss?

How desperately calm the landscapes were?
His heart, become a stone in the catapult
of his mind, could have struck the foolish adult

passions where murder and faith excluded each
other. Though eagles still hung like electric fans
in the sky and the rocks suggested permanence,

the blood in the earth was not poultry-yard slaughter.
The boy cushioned his heart in the moss
of withdrawal for his India and his youth were lost.

The picnic in Jammu

Uncle Ayub swung me round and round
till the horizon became a rail
banked high upon the Himalayas.
The trees signalled me past. I whistled,
shut my eyes through tunnels of the air.
The family laughed, watching me puff
out my muscles, healthily aggressive.

*This was late summer, before the snows
come to Kashmir, this was picnic time.*

Then, uncoupling me from the sky, he
plunged me into the river, himself
a bough with me dangling at its end.
I went purple as a plum. He reared
back and lowered the branch of his arm
to grandma who swallowed me with a kiss.
Laughter peeled away my goosepimples.

This was late summer, before the snows
come to Kashmir, this was picnic time.

After we'd eaten, he aimed grapes at
my mouth. I flung at him the shells of
pomegranates and ran off. He tracked
me down the river bank. We battled,
melon rind and apple core our arms.
'You two!' grandma cried. 'Stop fighting, you'll
tire yourselves to death!' We didn't listen.

This was late summer, before the snows
come to Kashmir and end children's games.

Decomposition

I have a picture I took in Bombay
of a beggar asleep on the pavement:
grey-haired, wearing shorts and a dirty shirt,
his shadow thrown aside like a blanket.

His arms and legs could be cracks in the stone,
routes for the ants' journeys, the flies' descents.
Brain-washed by the sun into exhaustion,
he lies veined into stone, a fossil man.

Behind him, there is a crowd passingly
bemused by a pavement trickster and quite
indifferent to this very common sight
of an old man asleep on the pavement.

I thought it then a good composition
and glibly called it *The Man in the Street*,
remarking how typical it was of
India that the man in the street lived there.

His head in the posture of one weeping
into a pillow chides me now for my
presumption at attempting to compose
art out of his hunger and solitude.

John Pepper Clark-Bekederemo (b 1935)

Clark-Bekederemo was born, like Gabriel Okara (see p. 90), in the Ijaw district
of Nigeria. He is well known as a poet, dramatist, and critic. He was for many
years Professor of English at the University of Lagos, and subsequently was the
artistic director of the Repertory Theatre in Lagos.

Ibadan

Ibadan,
          running splash of rust
and gold – flung and scattered
among seven hills like broken
china in the sun.

Night rain

What time of night it is
I do not know
Except that like some fish
Doped out of the deep
I have bobbed up bellywise
From stream of sleep
And no cocks crow.
It is drumming hard here
And I suppose everywhere
Droning with insistent ardour upon
Our roof thatch and shed
And through sheaves slit open
To lightning and rafters
I cannot quite make out overhead
Great water drops are dribbling
Falling like orange or mango
Fruits showered forth in the wind
Or perhaps I should say so
Much like beads I could in prayer tell

Them on string as they break
In wooden bowls and earthenware
Mother is busy now deploying
About our roomlet and floor.
Although it is so dark
I know her practised step as
She moves her bins, bags and vats
Out of the run of water
That like ants filing out of the wood
Will scatter and gain possession
Of the floor. Do not tremble then
But turn, brothers, turn upon your side
Of the loosening mats
To where the others lie.
We have drunk tonight of a spell
Deeper than the owl's or bat's
That wet of wings may not fly.
Bedraggled up on the iroko, they stand
Emptied of hearts, and
Therefore will not stir, no, not
Even at dawn for then
They must scurry in to hide.
So let us roll over on our back
And again roll to the beat
Of drumming all over the land
And under its ample soothing hand
Joined to that of the sea
We will settle to a sleep of the innocent and free.

Don Mattera (b 1935)

Mattera was born in what was then Western Native Township. Early on in his life
he played football for the Sophiatown African Morning Stars, and was the leader
of a gang called the Vultures. His political involvement in the 1970s led to his
being banned for nine years, for three of which he was under house arrest. See
Mongane Wally Serote's poem 'For Don M. – banned' (p. 185). He converted to
Islam, and works in journalism and as a community leader in Eldorado Park.

Let the children decide

Let us halt this quibbling
Of reform and racial preservation
Saying who belongs to which nation
And let the children decide
It is their world.

Let us burn our uniforms
Of old scars and grievances
And call back our spent dreams
And the relics of crass tradition
That hang on our malignant hearts
And let the children decide
For it IS their world

Remember

Remember to call at my grave
When freedom finally
Walks the land
That I may rise
To tread familiar paths
To see broken chains
Fallen prejudice
Forgotten injury
Pardoned pains.

And when my eyes have filled their sight
Do not run away for fright
If I crumble to dust again
It will only be the bliss
Of a long-awaited dream
That bids me rest
When freedom finally walks the land

Lucille Clifton (b 1936)

Clifton was born in New York, and studied at Howard College. She has worked as a teacher, a writer-in-residence, and a professor in a number of universities.

Miss Rosie

When I watch you
wrapped up like garbage
sitting, surrounded by the smell
of too old potato peels
or
when I watch you
in your old man's shoes
with the little toe cut out
sitting, waiting for your mind
like next week's grocery
I say
when I watch you
you wet brown bag of a woman
who used to be the best looking gal in Georgia
used to be called the Georgia Rose
I stand up
through your destruction
I stand up

Judith Rodriguez (b 1936)

Rodriguez was born in Perth, and teaches at the La Trobe University in Australia. Her collections of poems include *Nu-Plastic Fanfare Red* and *Water Life*.

How come the truck-loads?

Somehow the tutorial takes an unplanned direction:
anti-Semitism.
A scholastic devil advances the suggestion
that two sides can be found to every question:
Right.
Now, who's an anti-Semite?
One hand.
Late thirties, in the 1960s. Bland.

Let's see now; tell us, on what texts or Jews
do you base your views?
There was a landlord, from Poland, that I had.
Bad?
A shrug. Well, what did he do?
Pretty mean chasing up rent. Ah. Tough.
And who
else? No one else. One's enough.

Adam Small (b 1936)

Small was born in Wellington in the Cape, and grew up in Robertson and
Cape Town. He studied at the Universities of Cape Town, London and Oxford.
Having lectured in Philosophy at Fort Hare University, he was first Professor of
Philosophy and then Professor of Social Welfare at the University of the Western
Cape. He writes mainly in Afrikaans, occasionally in English.

O kroeskop!

Bushy head
so they call you
to insult you
bushy head
but bushy head
birds can nest in you
daily fly from you
and return to you
carrying home to you
in their wings for you
heaven;
have their young in you
hold their young in you

till they fly from you
and return to you
carrying home to you
in their wings for you
heaven

bushy head
so they call you
to insult you

bushy head
but bushy head
you can accommodate
heaven

Barry Feinberg (b 1938)

Feinberg was born in Germiston and educated at the Johannesburg School
of Art. He went into exile in 1961, and studied at the Slade Art School at the
University of London. He became Director of Publications for the International
Defence and Aid Fund, founded the ANC Cultural Ensemble, and edited a
collection of South African poems titled *Poets to the People*. In 1991 he returned
to South Africa and is now one of the directors of the Mayibuye Centre for
History and Culture at the University of the Western Cape.

In November 1965 Ian Smith and his Rhodesian Front declared Southern
Rhodesia independent of Britain in a Unilateral Declaration of Independence
(UDI). The consequence was the fifteen-year-long Second Chimurenga
(Struggle), which ended with the creation of the new independent Zimbabwe.

No cause for alarm

(On a statement by the Smith regime, July 1973)

A warning
in confidence
to tobacco growers
from Rhodesia owners
about invaders
who may wish
to eliminate you:

Maintain vigilance over your minions
keep compass on degree of turn out
watch for abnormal compound activity
check and double check loyalty
and test allegiance constantly.
In short
keep eyes peeled
for signs of grudge
grievance or latent agitation.
Employees are easily subverted
grudgeholders in particular

are easy meat for marauders.
Check and double check
all loiterers, malingerers
and squatters
for possible imposters.
By law only *your* natives
may live as your labour.
If dramatic change occurs
summon security forces.

Ten tips against slip-up
in case of terrorist attack
if carefully carried out
will fool all intruders:

1
To confuse observation
avoid obvious routine
vary your bed nightly
but not till servants
are out of sight.
Have houseboys return all keys
you may once have entrusted.

2
Essential poisons for crops
husbandry and irritating insects
including bathroom medications
must be collected
secured against servants
or safely thrown away.

3
Floodlights, though a comfort
can easily be spotted
by all types of terrorist
trained to make like moths at night.
Likewise, tallow or torches
can pinpoint your position.

4
When erected
security fences

electric or spiked
provide excellent protection
but *keep your children clear.*

5
Positioned on your perimeters
trip wires and man traps
are both deadly deterrents
but *remember to unman*
every morning.

6
In event of rocket attack
beware of external walls
but above all
don't stand behind your door
if knocked at night.

7
Liberate your livestock
let your dogs roam free
give geese maximum mobility
as an early warning system
but *bear in mind*
they may be used
as a ruse
to get at you.

8
Don't blunder out at a bark
or get up your gander
always creep with extreme caution
and beware of deep breathing.

9
If you trip your own wire
or trigger your traps
don't shoot or shout
when without light
hold your fire
as your spouse
might take your bullet
as a parting gift.

10
Though it's not our intention
to stir apprehension
nor create a state of alarm
you must now endeavour
to love your labour
for the sake of us all
and your farm.

Margaret Atwood (b 1939)

Attwood was born in Ottawa, and educated at the University of Toronto and at Harvard. She is Canada's best-known novelist and has also published a number of books of poems.

Woman skating

A lake sunken among
cedar and black spruce hills;
late afternoon.

On the ice a woman skating,
jacket sudden
red against the white,

concentrating on moving
in perfect circles.

> (actually she is my mother, she is
> over at the outdoor skating rink
> near the cemetery. On three sides
> of her there are streets of brown
> brick houses; cars go by; on the
> fourth side is the park building.
> The snow banked around the rink
> is grey with soot. She never skates
> here. She's wearing a sweater and
> faded maroon earmuffs, she has
> taken off her gloves)

Now near the horizon
the enlarged pink sun swings down.
Soon it will be zero.

With arms wide the skater
turns, leaving her breath like a diver's
trail of bubbles.

Seeing the ice
as what it is, water:
seeing the months
as they are, the years
in sequence occurring
underfoot, watching
the miniature human
figure balanced on steel
needles (those compasses
floated in saucers) on time
sustained, above
time circling: miracle

Over all I place
a glass bell

C J (Jonty) Driver (b 1939)

Driver was detained while he was the president of NUSAS, the National Union
of South African Students. After his release he went into exile in the United
Kingdom, and his passport was withdrawn while he was studying at Oxford
University. He was not allowed to return to South Africa for many years. He has
taught in various schools in the United Kingdom and Hong Kong, and is now
the principal of Wellington College. He has published four novels and a number
of collections of poems.

Well, goodbye

I'd been skirting it all day, what I'd say
At our last parting, at the aerodrome
(Our joking way of sharing older times
To use the older terms gone out of taste).
Of course we knew. At lunch I said something
Rather feeble about the next summer –
Already I had shifted hemispheres
And meant the summer on the northern side.

Of course we knew. This was to be our last
Goodbye. There would be no more coming back.
We've always hated partings, kept them brief,
Said, 'Well, goodbye,' touched quickly, turned and walked –
And don't look back.
                          And don't look back. And that
Was what we did; habit saved us from grief,
At least in public. It'd been just the same
Leaving home for boarding school, the long wait
On the hot platform, parents standing there,
And nothing left to say, not even
Silly things like, 'Now don't forget to write.'
We used to say to them: 'Goodbye and go.
We're on the train leaving any moment now.
Why wait? Why drag this parting out? We don't
Want to go away – you know. Any moment now
Mom will cry. Please go. Just say goodbye.'

The night he died, before I heard the news,
I woke at three, in a far country, far
Even from England. I had a dream.
I often dreamed of him, my small brother
With cancer, though never dead. But this time
He was dead. I was sure. I woke in tears.
He'd come to me, as ghost, or something else,
To let me know, with gruff laconic words:
'So this is where you are, in India…
I thought I'd better let you know. I'm off…'
And then, as usual, flatly, 'Well, goodbye.'
And I woke up, in grief but also joy,
Since wordless Simon had to go like that –
And going thus meant something else than death;
And I thought: but no one will believe this –
I should wake my hosts to say, 'My brother's dead;
I know he's dead,' before they telephone –
But I can't wake them now; it's three o'clock.
I'll tell them when we meet for morning tea.
I forgot, of course. One does. The call came
At breakfast time.

The 'miser' reference in the next poem is to a character in a nineteenth-century novel called *Silas Marner*, written by George Eliot. The recluse Silas has only one consolation: his growing pile of gold. We are used to the name Ruth, but no longer use the common noun 'ruth', meaning pity or compassion (that meaning survives in the negative adjective 'ruthless').

Grace and Silence

I thought his name was Silas: it suited
Since he collected junk of any kind
And stored it where my brother didn't keep
His car: junk of any kind – half a bike;
Old magazines; a broken saw; a lid
Without a pan, a handless clock, a lamp
My brother'd thrown away; broken glasses;
Cheque book stubs; shelves of any size;
All my brother's left-foot shoes. ('I s'pose,'
My brother said, 'there may be someone else
Who's lost the other leg, and needs those shoes –
Ol' Silas would find him.') He packed it up,
The junk I mean, in huge cardboard parcels
And monthly shipped them back, to the homeland,
Victorian dealer, Miser, Silas,
Quaint and kindly…
                                    'But you've got it wrong,'
My brother said. 'His name isn't Silas –
Silence, that's his name – parents called him that,
In hope he might have been, or since he was,
Like Ruth, I guess, or Hope, or Charity.'
Silence collected junk, for which he found
A use. Silence was always there. Silence
Took care. Silence shook hands and said, warmly,
'So you're the big brother, come from England,
Principal, of a high school, Simon said.'
(Not 'my baas', I was pleased to hear –
'I said he couldn't clean my car if he
"Baas"ed me,' my brother said, *sotto voce*.)
'I am very pleased to meet,' Silence said –
And I was very glad I'd left my bags inside.

Grace, on the other hand, came on Tuesdays
To do the ironing, and clean the flat
(Which needed it by then, I tell you man!).
She borrowed next week's wage to pay the school
Her children wouldn't go to, but he kept
A month or two ahead, and then forgot,
Although he said, 'I think she adds it up, and pays
In overtime.' He wasn't sure. 'Who cares?'
He said. 'It's just a kind of grown-up game
Between the three of us. When Silence needs
A bit of *"geld"*, he cleans my car, then says
"I cleaned your car because it needed me" –
It's a kind of local truce we've made,
I guess. I give them what they want, and they
Protect me, for a little time at least.
That's all I need, you see.'
                              Grace and Silence:
Grace does the dishes; Silence keeps the door.

Seamus Heaney (b 1939)

Heaney was born in Northern Ireland, and much of his early poetry concerns
the farmland environment of his childhood and youth. He was Professor of
Poetry at Oxford University from 1989 to 1994, and was awarded the Nobel Prize
for Literature in 1995.

Digging

Between my finger and my thumb
The squat pen rests; snug as a gun.

Under my window, a clean rasping sound
When the spade sinks into gravelly ground:
My father, digging. I look down

Till his straining rump among the flowerbeds
Bends low, comes up twenty years away
Stooping in rhythm through potato drills
Where he was digging.

The coarse boot nestled on the lug, the shaft
Against the inside knee was levered firmly.
He rooted out tall tops, buried the bright edge deep
To scatter new potatoes that we picked
Loving their cool hardness in our hands.

By God, the old man could handle a spade.
Just like his old man.

My grandfather cut more turf in a day
Than any other man on Toner's bog.
Once I carried him milk in a bottle
Corked sloppily with paper. He straightened up
To drink it, then fell to right away
Nicking and slicing neatly, heaving sods
Over his shoulder, going down and down
For the good turf. Digging.

The cold smell of potato mould, the squelch and slap
Of soggy peat, the curt cuts of an edge
Through living roots awaken in my head.
But I've no spade to follow men like them.

Between my finger and my thumb
The squat pen rests.
I'll dig with it.

Follower

My father worked with a horse-plough,
His shoulders globed like a full sail strung
Between the shafts and the furrow.
The horses strained at his clicking tongue.

An expert. He would set the wing
And fit the bright steel-pointed sock.
The sod rolled over without breaking.
At the headrig, with a single pluck

Of reins, the sweating team turned round
And back into the land. His eye
Narrowed and angled at the ground,
Mapping the furrow exactly.

I stumbled in his hob-nailed wake,
Fell sometimes on the polished sod;
Sometimes he rode me on his back
Dipping and rising to his plod.

I wanted to grow up and plough,
To close one eye, stiffen my arm.
All I ever did was follow
In his broad shadow round the farm.

I was a nuisance, tripping, falling,
Yapping always. But today
It is my father who keeps stumbling
Behind me, and will not go away.

The poet describes 'Station Island' as a 'sequence of dream encounters with familiar ghosts, set on Station Island on Lough Derg in County Donegal'.

Station Island section vii

I had come to the edge of the water,
soothed by just looking, idling over it
as if it were a clear barometer

or a mirror, when his reflection
did not appear but I sensed a presence
entering into my concentration

on not being concentrated as he spoke
my name. And though I was reluctant
I turned to meet his face and the shock

is still in me at what I saw. His brow
was blown open above the eye and blood
had dried on his neck and cheek. 'Easy now,'

he said, 'it's only me. You've seen men as raw
after a football match ... What time it was
when I was wakened up I still don't know

but I heard this knocking, knocking, and it
scared me, like the phone in the small hours,
so I had the sense not to put on the light

but looked out from behind the curtain.
I saw two customers on the doorstep
and an old landrover with the doors open

parked on the street so I let the curtain drop;
but they must have been waiting for it to move
for they shouted to come down into the shop.

She started to cry then and roll round the bed,
lamenting and lamenting to herself,
not even asking who it was. "Is your head

astray or what's come over you?" I roared, more
to bring myself to my senses
than out of any real anger at her

for the knocking shook me, the way they kept it up,
and her whingeing and half-screeching made it worse.
All the time they were shouting, "Shop!

Shop!" so I pulled on my shoes and a sportscoat
and went back to the window and called out,
"What do you want? Could you quieten the racket

or I'll not come down at all." "There's a child not well.
Open up and see what you have got – pills
or a powder or something in a bottle,"

one of them said. He stepped back off the footpath
so I could see his face in the street lamp
and when the other moved I knew them both.

But bad and all as the knocking was, the quiet
hit me worse. She was quiet herself now,
lying dead still, whispering to watch out.

At the bedroom door I switched on the light.
"It's odd they didn't look for a chemist.
Who are they anyway at this time of the night?"

she asked me, with the eyes standing in her head.
"I know them to see," I said, but something
made me reach and squeeze her hand across the bed

before I went downstairs into the aisle
of the shop. I stood there, going weak
in the legs. I remember the stale smell

of cooked meat or something coming through
as I went to open up. From then on
you know as much about it as I do.'

'Did they say nothing?' 'Nothing. What would they say?'
'Were they in uniform? Not masked in any way?'
'They were barefaced as they would be in the day,

shites thinking they were the be-all and the end-all.'
'Not that it is any consolation,
but they were caught,' I told him, 'and got jail.'

Big-limbed, decent, open-faced, he stood
forgetful of everything now except
whatever was welling up in his spoiled head,

beginning to smile. 'You've put on weight
since you did your courting in that big Austin
you got the loan of on a Sunday night.'

Through life and death he had hardly aged.
There always was an athlete's cleanliness
shining off him and except for the ravaged

forehead and the blood, he was still that same
rangy midfielder in a blue jersey
and starched pants, the one stylist on the team,

the perfect, clean, unthinkable victim.
'Forgive the way I have lived indifferent –
forgive my timid circumspect involvement,'

I surprised myself by saying. 'Forgive
my eye,' he said, 'all that's above my head.'
And then a stun of pain seemed to go through him

and he trembled like a heatwave and faded.

Eunice de Souza (b 1940)

De Souza was born into a Goan Catholic family in Mumbai (Bombay) in India. She is a graduate of the University of Bombay and Marquette University, Wisconsin, in the United States. She lectures in English literature at St Xavier's College in Mumbai. Several volumes of her poems have been published over the years.

De Souza Prabhu

No, I'm not going to
delve deep down and discover
I'm really de Souza Prabhu
even if Prabhu was no fool
and got the best of both worlds.
(Catholic Brahmin!
I can hear his chuckle still)

No matter that
my name is Greek
my surname Portuguese
my language alien.

There are ways
of belonging.

I belong with the lame ducks.

I heard it said
my parents wanted a boy.
I've done my best to qualify.
I hid the bloodstains
on my clothes
and let my breasts sag.
Words the weapon
to crucify.

Mbuyiseni Oswald Mtshali (b 1940)

Mtshali is known as the first black South African poet to publish a collection of poems written in English: *Sounds of a Cowhide Drum* appeared in 1972, and was, for many white South African readers, their first encounter with the township experience. The volume was a critical and commercial success, one of the very few South African books of poetry to have achieved this. A second volume in 1980 *Fire Flames* did not do well, and Mtshali has not published any poetry since then.

One of the points of interest in this next poem is the ambiguity of its final lines: what is the poet saying about this mother? and what is the tone of these lines? Look, also, at poems as different as Anne Stevenson's 'The victory' (p. 145) and Ingrid de Kok's two poems (p. 221).

An abandoned bundle

The morning mist
and chimney smoke
of White City Jabavu
flowed thick yellow
as pus oozing
from a gigantic sore.

It smothered our little houses
like fish caught in a net.

Scavenging dogs
draped in red bandanas of blood
fought fiercely
for a squirming bundle.

I threw a brick;
they bared fangs
flicked velvet tongues of scarlet
and scurried away,
leaving a mutilated corpse –
an infant dumped on a rubbish heap –
'Oh! Baby in the Manger
sleep well
on human dung.'

Its mother
had melted into the rays of the rising sun,
her face glittering with innocence
her heart as pure as untrampled dew.

Ama Ata Aidoo (b 1942)

Aidoo is one of Ghana's major poets. She has published plays and novels as well
as several collections of poems. She has frequently taught in American as well as
African universities. She has lived for some years in Zimbabwe, and visited
South Africa in 1994 to lecture on African literature and development.

'Amanfuo' means 'Citizens'.

From the only speech that was not delivered at the rally

Amanfuo,

just look at
us
                and
know
the full
extent of
your distress.

Between me
                and
the other candidate,
there's quite a lot to choose from:

an extra inch or so of
bones,
a few pounds' difference –
in weight.

Where onc was born is
most important.   Especially when
we
tell
you
so.

Do take note

                and

not forget
to give me your vote
along with your
                wife

I am your tribesman
            And

who else but I,
your own housefly,
can suck your
                    sores
to hurt the most?

Education too
must not be missed.

                Or

how could we who have the best
make you and them
who have the least
or none at all
look
small?

For the rest, dear countrymen,
we promise you
no success,
no prosperity.

Man must have something to live for.

We survive on our
failures.

As things
do stand,
I've missed more
chances
                than
I can count,
                or
wish to count.

So
Time gives
Me her
'Go-ahead'
to chop you small
before I'm dead.

Jeni Couzyn (b 1942)

Couzyn was born and educated in South Africa, then lived in the United Kingdom, then in different parts of Canada, and now is back in the United Kingdom. She has had a number of collections of poems published, including *Christmas in Africa*, *Life by Drowning* and *Monkey's Wedding*.

In the house of the father

Christmas, the turning time, the final reckoning and the
forgiveness, we rode towards each year, over humps of
bitterness, towards the father

omnipotent and bountiful night rider with his magical
reindeer and sack full of gifts –
you could rely on him always to be there when you got there

accept the culmination of your year in his lap
hear all, forgive with a wish, and let you
begin all over;

a time of reprieve and new resolutions, time when you could
believe in new beginnings, a time of peace and long
playtime. With a hand in the dark

it began before dawn. The sun would rise over the city
as we passed the last gold hills of the mine dumps. Always
I saw children leaping up them, and in my head, in golden depths

a heap of little skeletons. Then the long hot hours dreaming
through the dorps each its single tree and tin roofs blazing
each its lone dog barking and black silent men

propped on the verandah of the general store, drinking
lemonade. Endless car games, the singing game chanting every rhyme
    we knew
from ten green bottles to jesus loves me over the veld

to pass the time. At last, crossing, purple and lonely
the valley of a thousand hills, the tropical
deep smell of heavy flowers would glut the evening

and my father offered sixpence for the first to see the sea.
And there it was after a sudden unbending – that immense blue promise.
Then inland into the sugar cane in the deep of night

the rustle of dunes and the sugar cane fields
the farmers who kept pythons fifty feet long to keep the rats down
and at midnight

the cottage. O the damp smell of foliage, smell of salt
and the sea's heavy breathing in the night, stray cries
of live things, batswing, shadows, sleep, and a ring of mornings.

The snakes were the price. In their hundreds they inhabited
our world at christmas. They were the hazard
in the garden. And they were everywhere

tangled in undergrowth, slithering over your feet in the pathway
stretched across doorways in the sun
lurking under the banana plant and nesting in the luckybean tree

they were everywhere, everywhere. And happiness was everywhere
in the father's time, who came down from heaven
in his red dressing gown and my father's shoes at the appointed time

cottonwool beard lopsided across his grin
his arms full of parcels.
His was the future that always came, keeping its promise.

In the house of the father the year would turn
a flower full blown, shedding its petals.
Glistened in your hand a free gift, a clean seed.

Dilemma of a telephone operator

which department please
    childrens
which department madam
fire police or ambulance
tell me quickly
    the emergency department
yes but which section? tell me
at once what happened and I'll
put you through
    he died whimpering all night
    this doctor won't help him
is he completely dead
    utterly

then you must call the funeral men
they will bury his body
>   don't you understand this is
>   an emergency
its not our kind of emergency dear
>   but you are 999
yes but we have no department as such
to cope with death
>   help me
I'm sorry
>   help me help me
I'm very sorry. I truly am sorry
>   help
O dear try your local church try
the mental health clinic try
the citizens advice bureau
>   I want him alive again I want
>   these men to go away
I'm not bloody God. Christ what do you
expect me to do?
>   if you could see the way he's
>   lying there without moving
>   you'd think of something

Micere Githae Mugo (b 1942)

Mugo was born in Kenya. She was educated at the Universities of Makerere, Nairobi, and New Brunswick, Canada. In 1982 she became Professor of Literature at the University of Zimbabwe. She has published criticism, poems, and plays.

Where are those songs?

Where are those songs
my mother and yours
always sang
fitting rhythms
to the whole
vast span of life?

What was it again
they sang
>   harvesting maize, threshing millet, storing the grain ...

What did they sing
bathing us, rocking us to sleep ...
and the one they sang
stirring the pot
(swallowed in parts by choking smoke)?

What was it
the woods echoed
as in long file
my mother and yours and all the women on our ridge
beat out the rhythms
        trudging gaily
        as they carried
        piles of wood
        through those forests
        miles from home

What song was it?

And the row of bending women
hoeing our fields
to what beat
did they
break the stubborn ground
as they weeded
our *shambas*?

What did they sing
at the ceremonies
        child-birth
        child-naming
        second birth
        initiation ...?
how did they trill the *ngemi*
What was
the warriors' song?
how did the wedding song go?
sing me
the funeral song.
What do you remember?

Sing
        I have forgotten
        my mother's song

      my children
      will never know.
This I remember:
Mother always said
      sing child sing
      make a song
      and sing
      beat out your own rhythms
      the rhythms of your life
      but make the song soulful
      and make life
      sing

Sing daughter sing
around you are
uncountable tunes
some sung
others unsung
sing them
to your rhythms
observe
listen
absorb
soak yourself
bathe
in the stream of life
      and then sing
      sing
      simple songs
      for the people
      for all to hear
      and learn
      and sing
      with you

Nikki Giovanni (b 1943)

Giovanni was born, as the next poem indicates, in Tennessee in the United
States. She was for many years the leading figure in female African American
writing. She has been a poet, recording artist and lecturer, and has a number
of honorary doctorates from universities. She has published over ten collections
of her poems.

Knoxville, Tennessee

I always like summer
best
you can eat fresh corn
from daddy's garden
and okra
and greens
and cabbage
and lots of
barbecue
and buttermilk
and homemade ice-cream
at the church picnic
and listen to
gospel music
outside
at the church
homecoming
and go to the mountains with
your grandmother
and go barefooted
and be warm
all the time
not only when you go to bed
and sleep

Nikki Rosa

childhood memories are always a drag
if you're Black
you always remember things like living in Woodlawn
with no inside toilet
and if you become famous or something
they never talk about how happy you were to have
your mother
all to yourself and
how good the water felt when you got your bath
from one of those
big tubs that folk in chicago barbeque in
and somehow when you talk about home
it never gets across how much you

understood their feelings
as the whole family attended meetings about Hollydale
and even though you remember
your biographers never understand
your father's pain as he sells his stock
and another dream goes
And though you're poor it isn't poverty that
concerns you
and though they fought a lot
it isn't your father's drinking that makes any difference
but only that everybody is together and you
and your sister have happy birthdays and very good
Christmases
and I really hope no white person ever has cause
to write about me
because they'll never understand
Black love is Black wealth and they'll
probably talk about my hard childhood
and never understand that
all the while I was quite happy

Shakuntala Hawoldar (b 1944)

Hawoldar was born in Mumbai (Bombay), India. At the age of 23 she emigrated
to Mauritius, where she married a Mauritian and worked in the Ministry of
Education and Culture. After her divorce, she and her three children moved to
India. Three collections of her verse have been published.

Destruction

I do not know what has destroyed you,
Maybe it was too much of loving
Or too little.
Both strangely have the same face – mine
When I look upon my hands
That have caressed you,
Untied corded muscles of pain
On cool sheets
Spreading my hair upon your limbs
To inflame them,
How would I know

That I could darken your eyes
And bring down the blinds
Upon your soul,
Hurt you by wordless thought
Scoop out warmth from your centre,
Leave dark regions of despair –
I do not know how I've destroyed you
Maybe it was too much of loving
Or too little

To my little girl

She was little,
She did not know the use of shoes;
I warned her of the brambles in the bush, in the briars,
She laughed trampling my words,
Briars, under naked feet;
She knows, I sighed
There are no shoes which she can wear for briars, brambles,
For she has seen me bleed,
Seen me bruised,
With my feet clothed and covered.

Ben J Langa (1944–84)

Langa was brought up in KwaMashu in Durban, and became an activist in what was then called Natal. He was murdered in 1984 by Umkhonto we Sizwe agents because he was suspected of being a National Party government spy. In its first submission to the Truth and Reconciliation Commission, the ANC admitted that it had been tricked by a double agent into ordering Langa's death.

For my brothers (Mandla and Bheki) in exile

You have seen part of the world
Met some very nice people
Experienced the hardships of fresh air
Longed for the warm home-fires
Around which we sat on winter nights
Listening to pa tell us stories
Or reading passages from the Bible.

Those were the days, my brother Mandla,
Some days they were, my brother Bheki.
Do you remember those days?
When we were young and happy together
Playing cops and robbers, hide and seek,
Pinching bottoms whilst in hiding –
Young and happy together?
One day it would rain
And before the night was out
We'd be carrying brooms, sacks and buckets,
Urging the water out of our house.
You do remember those days?

Maybe I do not know where you are.
You left in the stealth of the night
Maybe hiked miles in fear but determined
To finally reach new worlds unknown.
Some days I happen to clean house
Exploring every nook and cranny.
I find here and there memories of our youth
Written on scraps of black and white photos.
I shake my head in pain of loss,
Say to myself, 'Gone are those days.'

The old woman is still around, brothers,
Heavy creases run down her mahogany face;
They are dry rivulets opened by heavy rains of pain.
At night, alone in the vaults of darkness,
She prays. In her prayer she talks about you.
Mama cries at night – by day she laughs,
Tending sisters' small children.
I know she longs to catch but one glimpse
Of her flesh and blood. Of her own womb.
Sometimes she talks about it,
Swallowing lumps, hiding tears behind eyes.
Mama is strong. Very tough. She was carved in teak.
In the evenings when we're together, she sometimes
Sings the songs we used to sing together.
Then she goes to sleep. I wonder if she'll sleep.

On Xmas Day mama makes custard and jelly,
Reminds us of how we all looked forward to Xmas
Because that was about the only day

We ever tasted custard and jelly.
Big bowls of jelly would be made
Then taken to the kindly butcher
(Remember, we didn't have a fridge).
Some time before our big meal
She'd send one of us to collect the bowls.
I remember we would handle those bowls gingerly
As though our whole life depended on them.

I do not know, maybe, what you're doing out there.
I know you're alive, yet longing for the home country.
You loved this country deeply,
So much that you could leave only to come back
When it has gained more sense.
Our neighbours (the ones you knew so well) are still there.
We meet at the tap (it's still outside) and chat.
They ask about you. They care about you.
Those days you do remember.

In all our pain and agony we rejoice,
For the tensile steel strength of our souls
Transcends borders and boundaries.
However far apart our bodies may be
Our souls are locked together in a perpetual embrace.

Jack Mapanje (b 1944)

Mapanje was born in Kadango village in Malawi, and has lived in Malawi and in
the United Kingdom. His first collection of poems *Of Chameleons and Gods* was
published in 1981. On its second reprint in 1985, it was banned in Malawi, and in
1987 he was arrested and then detained in Mikuyu Maximum Detention Centre
near Zomba for three years and eight months. No charges were ever brought
against him. He was released in May 1991, following pressure from fellow writers
internationally. He now lives in the United Kingdom with his wife and three
children, and has published a collection of poems called *The Chattering Wagtails
of Mikuyu Prison*.

Your tears still burn at my handcuffs (1991)

After that millet beer you brewed, mother
(In case Kadango Mission made something of
Another lake-son for the village to strut

About!); and after that fury with Special
Branch when I was brought home handcuffed –
'How dare you scatter this peaceful house?

What has my son done? Take me instead, you
Insensitive men!' you challenged their threat
To imprison you too as you did not '*stop*

Your gibberish!' – After that constant care
Mother, I expected you to show me the rites
Of homing in of this political prisoner,

Perhaps with ground herbal roots dug by
Your hand and hoe, poured in some clay pot
Of warm water for me to suffuse, perhaps

With your usual wry smile about the herbs
You wish your mother had told you about.
Today, as I invent my own cleansing rites

At this return of another fugitive, without
Even dead roots to lean on, promise to bless
These lit candles I place on your head and

Your feet, accept these bended knees, this
Lone prayer offered among these tall unknown
Graveyard trees, this strange requiem mustered

From the tattered Catholic Choir of Dembo
Village. You gave up too early, mother: two
More months, and I'd have told you the story

Of some Nchinji upstart who tamed a frog at
Mikuyu Prison, how he gave it liberty to invite
Fellow frogs to its wet niche, dearly feeding

Them insects and things; but how one day,
After demon bruises, his petulant inmate
Threw boiling water at the niche, killing

Frog and visitor. And I hoped you'd gather
Some tale for me too, one better than your
Grand-daughter's about how you told her she

Would not find you on her return from school
That day. But we understand, after so many
Pointless sighs about your son's expected

Release, after the village ridicule of your
Rebellious breasts and sure fatigue of your
Fragile bones, your own minders, then your

Fear for us when the release did finally come –
You'd propose yet another exile, without you –
We understand you had to go, to leave us space

To move. Though now, among the gentle friends
Of these Jorvik walls, I wonder why I still
Glare at your tears burning at my handcuffs.

Mongane Wally Serote (b 1944)

Serote was born in Sophiatown and attended school in Alexandra. In 1969 he
was detained for nine months and released without being charged. After a
period of study at Columbia University in the United States, he went into exile,
first in Botswana, then in the United Kingdom, where he became the head of the
ANC's Department of Arts and Culture. He returned to South Africa in 1990
and is now a Member of Parliament. He has published many volumes of poems,
one novel, and one book of literary essays. He was awarded the Ingrid Jonker
Prize in 1975 and the Ad Donker Prize for his outstanding contribution to the
literature of the seventies.

In the poem that follows, Serote's strong Black Consciousness advocacy
in the 1970s is expressed in the people's aspirations, and through their
achievements in the arts. 'Mankunku' is the saxophonist Winston Mankunku
Ngozi. 'Dumile' is the sculptor and painter Dumile Feni. 'Thoko' is the singer
Thoko Thomo, who sang with Sophiatown's LoSix and was famous for her
rendition of the song 'Skokiaan'.

Hell, well, heaven

I do not know where I have been,
But Brother,
I know I'm coming.
I do not know where I have been,
But Brother,
I know I heard the call.
Hell! where I was I cried silently

Yet I sat there until now.
I do not know where I have been,
But Brother,
I know I'm coming:
I come like a tide of water now,
But Oh! There's sand beneath me!
I do not know where I have been
To feel so weak, Heavens! so weary.
But Brother,
Was that Mankunku's horn?
Hell! my soul aches like a body that has been beaten,
Yet I endured till now.
I do not know where I have been,
But Brother,
I know I'm coming.
I do not know where I have been,
But Brother I come like a storm over the veld,
And Oh! there are stone walls before me!
I do not know where I have been
To have fear so strong like the whirlwind (will it be that brief?)
But Brother,
I know I'm coming.
I do not know where I have been,
But Brother,
Was that Dumile's figure?
Hell, my mind throbs like a heart beat, there's no peace;
And my body of wounds – when will they be scars? –
Yet I can still walk and work and still smile.
I do not know where I have been
But Brother,
I know I'm coming.
I do not know where I have been,
But Brother,
I have a voice like the lightning-thunder over the mountains.
But Oh! there are copper lightning conductors for me!
I do not know where I have been
To have despair so deep and deep and deep
But Bother,
I know I'm coming.
I do not know where I have been
But Brother,
Was that Thoko's voice?
Hell, well, Heavens!

The actual dialogue

Do not fear Baas.
It's just that I appeared
And our faces met
In this black night that's like me.
Do not fear –
We will always meet
When you do not expect me.
I will appear
In the night that's black like me.
Do not fear –
Blame your heart
When you fear me –
I will blame my mind
When I fear you
In the night that's black like me.
Do not fear Baas,
My heart is vast as the sea
And your mind as the earth.
It's awright Baas,
Do not fear.

'Don M.' is the poet Don Mattera (see p. 152). When the National Party
government banned someone, one of the stipulations was that nothing that
person said or wrote could be quoted, printed or published. The effect of
banning on a poet is easy to imagine. Is this poem separable from its title? Is it
a nature poem? Or a political poem?

For Don M. – banned

it is a dry white season
dark leaves don't last, their brief lives dry out
and with a broken heart they dive down gently headed for the earth,
not even bleeding.
it is a dry white season brother,
only the trees know the pain as they still stand erect
dry like steel, their branches dry like wire,
indeed, it is a dry white season
but seasons come to pass.

Alice Walker (b 1944)

Walker is best known for her Pulitzer Prize-winning novel *The Color Purple*. She
has also published a number of collections of poems, including *'Good Night, Willie
Lee, I'll See You in the Morning'* and *Horses Make a Landscape Look More Beautiful*.

Once section v

It is true –
I've always loved
the daring
            ones
Like the black young
man
Who tried
to crash
All barriers
at once,
        wanted to
swim
At a white
beach (in Alabama)
Nude.

Once section vii

            I
      never liked
      white folks
        really
          it
    happened quite
      suddenly
        one
        day
      A pair of
      amber
       eyes
        I
       think
        he
       had.

In the extract that follows, Alice Walker uses the word 'Negro', not a word African Americans would use today. The poem was first published in 1968.

Once section viii

I *don't* think
　　integration
　　　entered
　　　　into it
　　　　　officer

You see
　　there was
　　　this little
　　　　Negro
　　　　girl
Standing here
　　alone
　　and her
　　　mother
　　　　went into
that store
　　　there

then –
　　there came by
this little boy
　　here
without his
　　mother
& eating
　　an
ice cream cone
– see there it is –
　　strawberry

Anyhow

　　　　and the little
　　　　girl was
　　　　hungry
　　　　and
　　　　stronger
　　　　than

> the little
> boy –

Who is too
> *fat*
> really,

> anyway.

The kiss

i was kissed once
by a beautiful man
all blond and
> czech
riding through bratislava
on a motor bike
screeching 'don't yew let me fall off heah naow!'

the funny part was
he spoke english
and setting me gallantly
on my feet
kissed me for
not anyhow *looking*
like aunt jemima.

Wendy Cope (b 1945)

Cope was born in Kent, educated at Oxford, and lives in London. Specializing
in light satirical verse, she has published *Making Cocoa for Kingsley Amis* and
Serious Concerns.

Bloody men

Bloody men are like bloody buses –
You wait for about a year
And as soon as one approaches your stop
Two or three others appear.

You look at them flashing their indicators,
Offering you a ride.

You're trying to read the destinations,
You haven't much time to decide.

If you make a mistake, there is no turning back.
Jump off, and you'll stand there and gaze
While the cars and the taxis and lorries go by
And the minutes, the hours, the days.

Another Christmas poem

Bloody Christmas, here again.
Let us raise a loving cup:
Peace on earth, goodwill to men,
And make them do the washing-up.

Serious concerns

'*She is witty and unpretentious, which is both her strength and her limitation.*'
   (Robert O'Brien in the *Spectator*, 25.10.86)

I'm going to try and overcome my limitation –
Away with sloth!
Now should I work at being less witty? Or more pretentious?
Or both?

'*They (Roger McGough and Brian Patten) have something in common with her, in that they all write to amuse.*' (Ibid.)

Write to amuse? What an appalling suggestion!
I write to make people anxious and miserable and to worsen their
   indigestion.

Jennifer Davids (b 1945)

Davids was born in Cape Town and trained at the Hewat Teacher Training
College. She has taught and lived in London as well as in Cape Town.
   Compare this poem with Grace Nichols's 'Praise song for my mother' (p. 219).

Poem for my mother

That isn't everything, you said
on the afternoon I brought a poem
to you hunched over the washtub

with your hands
the shrivelled
burnt granadilla
skin of your hands
covered by foam.

And my words
slid like a ball
of hard blue soap
into the tub
to be grabbed and used by you
to rub the clothes.

A poem isn't all
there is to life, you said
with your blue-ringed gaze
scanning the page
once looking over my shoulder
and back at the immediate
dirty water

and my words
being clenched
smaller and
smaller.

Mafika Pascal Gwala (b 1946)

Gwala grew up in Verulam and in Vryheid in KwaZulu-Natal. He has worked as a legal clerk, a factory-worker, a teacher, and an industrial relations officer. He has had two volumes of poems published: *Jol'iinkomo* and *No More Lullabies*.

One small boy longs for summer

(for Bill Naughton)

The kettle hisses
Mother moves about the kitchen
sliding from corner to corner.
The fire from the stove
pierces into the marrow.

And mother pushing towards the stove
warns of the steam.
My young brother, Thamu, jerks my arm
violently: Stop leaning on me, your elbow
has sunk into my thigh.
          Apology
                    I wasn't aware.

The kettle sings
              Some distant far-away song?
Mother picks it up
with an almost tender care.
Sets me thinking of a war-picture
The actor carefully setting the charge
and smiling all the time
              I'll also be a soldier
when I'm old – why, Uncle Shoba was one.
Father drops the paper on the table
He comes to join us
              – staring coldly round.
It's no frown really,
But he's grinding his jaws.
              Maybe it's the July
Handicap.

The kettle purrs now
Steam is escaping; it kisses the ceiling
and vanishes. Mother is pouring the violent waters
into the coffee-jug. Coffee.
Yes, I need some coffee – a mug of hot coffee.
Very rousing.
We can't play outside – I must not go, I know
              How we danced in the rain. We are so tired
of the winter: It's so dingy outside.
We can't play inside – I'm so tied up.
It's so boring, I feel like bursting into
a cracking laughter; but father,
he'll go mad.
It's so steamy inside
I feel I could bite the walls down.
If only it makes the winter pass.

'Dompas' was the slang-word for the pass that all black African people had to carry at all times. Not to be able to produce your pass on demand was a criminal offence. The word is either the Afrikaans for 'stupid pass' or is derived from the word 'domicile', officialese for 'place of residence'. Of course, it ends up a clever pun on both. (See also James Matthews's poem on p. 121 and Stan Motjuwadi's poem on p. 130.) A 'kwela-kwela' was the slang-word for a police pick-up van, from the Nguni verb *khwela*, which means to climb or to mount.

Kwela-ride

Dompas!
I looked back
Dompas!
I went through my pockets
Not there.

They bit into my flesh (handcuffs).

Came the kwela-kwela
We crawled in.
The young men sang.
In that dark moment

It all became familiar.

Caroline Halliday (b 1947)

Halliday was born and lives in the United Kingdom. She has published novels, children's books, and a collection of poems.

ode to my daughter's plimsolls and the mess in her room

ode to my daughter's plimsolls,
and the mess in her room.
and her feet,
her toes one by one,
in my fingers,
ode to every part of her
the hair on her neck
the curl in her hair

the seriousness of her going to school
and teaching her to cross the road.
The time to write it
the time to notice it.
Notice her.
The time before she goes,
bright brown eyes.

She made me a cup of nettle tea,
'don't come out here till I say so'
and 'a touch of luxury'
she called it –
a green and gold tea cup,
and a saucer,
sipping thin green tea
she made for me.

Charles Mungoshi (b 1947)

Mungoshi was born in Manyene near Chivhu in Zimbabwe. He has worked
as a research assistant for the Forestry Commission, as a clerk in a bookshop,
and as a director of a publishing house. He has been writer-in-residence at the
University of Zimbabwe. He has published novels, short stories and a collection
of poems.

Read this poem side-by-side with Chenjerai Hove's 'You will forget' (p. 233).

If you don't stay bitter for too long

If you don't stay bitter
and angry for too long
you might finally salvage
something useful
from the old country

a lazy half sleep summer afternoon
for instance, with the whoof-whoof
of grazing cattle in your ears
tails swishing, flicking flies away
or the smell of newly turned soil
with birds hopping about
in the wake of the plough
in search of worms

or the pained look of your father
a look that took you all these years
and lots of places to understand

the bantering tone you used with your
grandmother and their old laugh
that said nothing matters but death

If you don't stay bitter
and angry for too long
and have the courage to go back
you will discover that the autumn smoke
writes different more helpful messages
in the high skies of the old country.

Sitting on the balcony

Sitting on the balcony
fingering a glass of beer
I have bought without
any intention to drink –
I see a little boy
poking for something
in a refuse dump –
looking for a future?
I am afraid, the stars say
your road leads to another
balcony just like this one
where you will sit fingering
a beer you have bought without
any intention to drink.

Niyi Osundare (b 1947)

Osundare was born in Nigeria. He won the Commonwealth Poetry Prize in
1986, the Cadbury Poetry Prize in 1989, and the Noma Award for Publishing in
Africa in 1991. With a BA degree from the University of Ibadan, Nigeria, an MA
from the University of Leeds, and a PhD from York University, Canada, he now
teaches English at the University of Ibadan.

Read this poem together with Lawrence Ferlinghetti's 'Constantly risking
absurdity' (p. 81) and Denise Levertov's 'The secret' (p. 98).

The poet

is not a gadfly
stinging putrefying carcasses
a
lone
in garbage lanes
no closet ink
can wash soiled streets
without the detergent
of collective action

is not a maverick
self-
consciously
deaf
to the homing whistle
through frayed jeans
can be seen, threadbare,
the flimsy texture
of feigning rebels

is not a prophet,
God's hollow ventriloquist,
auguring past futures
in dated tongues
the poet's eyes are washed
in the common spring
though seeing beyond
the hazy horizon
of lowering skies

The poet's pen is
the cactus by the stream
(shorn of its forbidding thorns)
each stem a nib
towards the field of action
its sap the ink of succour
when doubt's drought
assaults the well

Who says the poet
should leave the muck

unraked?
in a land of choking mud
how can the poet
strut
clean
in feathered sandals
and
pretend to the world
he never smells?

Achmat Dangor (b 1948)

Dangor was born in Johannesburg. He was a banned person for five years in the
seventies. In 1980 he won the Mofolo-Plomer Prize for his collection of stories
Waiting for Leila. He has published two collections of poems.

Paradise

Oh paradise,
cool paradise of Africa
your sea roars
like the restless roots
of our lives

and yet does not give life
to the dreams
of the people
you have forgotten.

Here, around me,
they destroy my city.
District Six,
they dismantle you
– stone by stone –
rock of my history.

On the walls
of my last refuge
cockroaches run
secretive and quiet,
an omen:
love and hope

that will have to
be hidden in darkness.

Somewhere in the twilight
a banjo trills, somewhere
on an overgrown terrace
people sing and people laugh,
the human voices of every day.

Oh paradise, cool paradise
of Africa,
what memories you recreate.

Oh why, why do you
tighten the chains?

Chris Zithulele Mann (b 1948)

Mann was born in Port Elizabeth, and educated at the Universities of the
Witwatersrand, Oxford (where he won the Newdigate Prize for Poetry) and
London. He taught for some time in Swaziland, then at Rhodes University, and
worked for the Valley Trust, a medical and agricultural development scheme in
KwaZulu-Natal. He has now returned to Grahamstown.

To Lucky with his guitar on a Grahamstown street

Here comes Lucky, the tallest of the tall;
born in PE; raised on a farm; not young
(nineteen); hardly been to school (no money);
can't find a job (no schooling); clouds of
brisk-eyed sparrows perch inside his guitar.

So here's Lucky, Coolhand Lucky the Tall;
Sunday afternoon; easing into town;
hasn't a word (drifting over New Street);
nothing to tell us (tapping the pavement);
but Coolhand riffs; zig-zag bass; stringshine chords.

And here's a car; a Chevvy; it's slowing,
it's parking. Nope. The missus is waving.
She's scared. Nope, she's angry; she has something
to say, yes, she's rolling down the window.
Lady? 'What are you kaffirs doing in town?'

Silence; the tar's wet; a truck bakes and ticks.
For Christ's sake, say something! You're the tallest,
Lucky, give it to her! Stupid old bitch.
Here it comes … Nope. Coolhand won't stop riffing.
The notes fly up like sparrows (for today).

In praise of the shades

Hitching across a dusty plain last June,
down one of those deadstraight platteland roads,
I met a man with rolled-up khakhi sleeves,
who told me his faults, and then his beliefs.
It's amazing, some people discuss more
with hitchhikers than even their friends.

His bakkie rattled a lot on the ruts,
so I'm not exactly sure what he said.
Anyway, when he'd talked about his church,
and when the world had changed from mealie-stalks
to sunflowers, which still looked green and firm,
he lowered his voice, and spoke about his shades.

This meant respect, I think, not secrecy.
He said he'd always asked them to guide him,
and that, even in the city, they did.
He seemed to me a gentle balanced man,
and I was sorry to stick my kitbag
onto the road again and say goodbye.

When you are alone and brooding deeply,
do all your teachers and loved ones desert you?
Stand on a road when the fence is whistling.
You say, 'It's the wind,' and if the dust swirls,
'Wind again,' although you never see it.
The shades work like the wind, invisibly.

And they have always been our companions,
dressed in the flesh of the children they reared,
gossiping away from the books they left,
a throng who even in the strongest light

are whispering, 'You are not what you are,
remember us, then try to understand.'

They come like pilgrims from the hazy seas
which shimmer at the borders of a dream,
not such spirits that they can't be scolded,
not such mortals that they can be profaned,
for scolding them, we honour each other,
and honouring them, we perceive ourselves.

When all I ever hear about these days
is violence, injustice, and despair,
or worse than that, humourless theories
to rescue us all from our human plight,
those moments in a bakkie on a plain
make sunflowers from a waterless world.

Epiphanies

[handwritten annotation:] Manifestation "of Christ to Magi" "a superhuman being"

1

If suffering, its persistence
is a mystery,
then so is joy.

Waking at dawn I found its music
drenching me utterly,

and couldn't convey
more than a trace of it,

a man with headphones, stepping out a subway
suddenly
leaping with a laugh in the air.

2

Whoever grew wise without sorrow?

Whoever loved
unless they trusted enough to bleed?

And who understood
till they'd shivered in fright at their ignorance?

3

Like dew
smoking off the bumpers of parked cars

such epiphanies
from time to momentary time
glisten,

then evaporate.

The homecoming

Let me try once again to convey what happened:

It's fairly late one summer evening
the sky beyond the garage
dark blue above a band of orange and deepening.

I've climbed out the car
stiff and tired from driving through rush-hour
and soured by the news on the radio.

The front door opens from the inside
and all at once
I'm sitting with my case on the threshold
a noisy and exuberant child
bouncing excitedly on each knee
embracing and being embraced
smelling the newly washed hair of their heads.

Albeit briefly
there seems to be nothing but happiness in the world.

Donald Parenzee (b 1948)

Parenzee grew up in Woodstock in Cape Town. He studied architecture, and
now teaches at the Peninsula Technikon.

Feeding

Your hands, especially,
feeding a bird,
finding the strand
of a slipknot

fixing

bait

flexing and

        casting

           out

their messages

in gut and sun

especially,
they
sing,
and what I catch
I know
as fact.

Your fingers speak
their own story.
Mine behave like slaves
to thought
and have been trained to tend
the burnished words of centuries and so

I feed
on your hands
especially.

Then the children decided

Then the children decided that
decades of words
having covered their pages,
grown from the spines
of decaying texts,
nourished on brain,
singed into skin,
that centuries
of so much print
would be edited,

censored,

burnt, if necessary
to free the heart
of the problem, and soon,
headless
screaming vowels,
dismembered paragraphs,
the bodies of essays,
whole crusts of theses,
littered the playgrounds, decaying
like the entrails of statutes

and rearing
like some statue of liberty,
the heart,
stripped of skin,
pumped its desperate slogans
into the fetid air.

18 June 1980

Ntozake Shange (b 1948)

Shange was born Paulette Williams in Trenton, New Jersey. She changed her
name in reaction against her Western roots. She studied at Barnard College
and at the University of California, Los Angeles. Her first major work was
a performance piece – she called it a 'choreopoem' – called *for colored girls
who have considered suicide when the rainbow is enuf.*

Lady in red

without any assistance or guidance from you
i have loved you assiduously for 8 months 2 wks & a day
i have been stood up four times
i've left 7 packages on yr doorstep
forty poems 2 plants & 3 handmade notecards i left
town so i cd send to you have been no help to me
on my job
you call at 3:00 in the mornin on weekdays
so i cd drive 27 ½ miles cross the bay before i go to work
charmin charmin
but you are of no assistance
i want you to know
this waz an experiment
to see how selfish i cd be
if i wd really carry on to snare a possible lover
if i waz capable of debasin my self for the love of another
if i cd stand not being wanted
when i wanted to be wanted
& i cannot
so
with no further assistance & no guidance from you
i am endin this affair

this note is attached to a plant
i've been waterin since the day i met you
you may water it
yr damn self

John Agard (b 1949)

Agard was born in Guyana in the Caribbean, and moved to the United Kingdom
in 1977. Among his books of poems are *Shoot Me With Flowers* and *Limbo
Dancer in Dark Glasses*.

Half-caste

Excuse me
standing on one leg
I'm half-caste

Explain yuself
wha yu mean
when yu say half-caste
yu mean when picasso
mix red an green
is a half-caste canvas/
explain yuself
wha yu mean
when yu say half-caste
yu mean when light an shadow
mix in de sky
is a half-caste weather/
well in dat case
england weather
nearly always half-caste
in fact some o dem cloud
half-caste till dem overcast
so spiteful dem dont want de sun pass
ah rass/
explain yuself
wha yu mean
when yu say half-caste
yu mean tchaikovsky
sit down at dah piano
an mix a black key
wid a white key
is a half-caste symphony/

Explain yuself
wha yu mean
Ah listening to yu wid de keen
half of mih ear
Ah looking at yu wid de keen
half of mih eye
an when I'm introduced to yu
I'm sure you'll understand
why I offer yu half-a-hand
an when I sleep at night
I close half-a-eye
consequently when I dream
I dream half-a-dream
an when moon begin to glow
I half-caste human being

cast half-a-shadow
but yu must come back tomorrow

wid de whole of yu eye
an de whole of yu ear
an de whole of yu mind

an I will tell yu
de other half
of my story

Rainbow

When you see
de rainbow
you know
God know
wha he doing –
one big smile
across the sky –
I tell you
God got style
the man got style

When you see
raincloud pass
and de rainbow
make a show
I tell you
is God doing
limbo
the man doing
limbo

But sometimes
you know
when I see
de rainbow
so full of glow
& curving
like she bearing child
I does want know
if God
ain't a woman

If that is so
the woman got style
man she got style

Shabbir Banoobhai (b 1949)

Banoobhai was born in Durban. He was for some time a lecturer at the
University of Durban Westville. He now lives and works in Cape Town.

you cannot know the fears i have

you cannot know the fears i have
as i think about you

i fear that i shall live only at your laughter
lie awake long nights while you sleep
so loneliness does not trouble you
nor hunger, nor thirst

overwhelm your waking world with wonder
with the music of other worlds, your earlier home
read to you poems written the night before
while you smile bewildered

or just when my very breathing begins to depend on you
even as your tiny fingers close around mine
some insensitive thing
crushes your butterfly spirit

shadows of a sun-darkened land
flow over you
and the eclipse
closes your eyes

i cannot live with the thought of having you, loving you
any other way
a day without such care
has no meaning

we shall find for you a name
your name shall bring light

by your own definition

by your own definition
i drink too deeply
the blood of roses

> lean on a leaf
> for comfort

> mistake mysteriously
> a thorn for a star

when the world curls itself
around my fingers
seas gather in my palms
trees sustain the sky

> my life lifts to loving
> love leaps to living

> and without words i strive to answer
> questions you have never asked

oh making you understand
is like trying to crush
the skull of a mountain

The author gives this note to the poem from which the following extracts are taken: 'Muhammad Iqbal (1873-1938) was born in Sialkot, Pakistan. He was a poet and a philosopher whose main source of inspiration was the Quran and who endeavoured in his work to show the excellence of the Islamic way of life. He kindled the movement that ultimately gave rise to the Islamic Republic of Pakistan.'

From Iqbal, it is winter here still

Iqbal, it is winter here still
It's been like this ever since you went away
The season is slow in turning
We have lost all sense of time
We have barricaded our doors against the wind and cold
We have barricaded our hearts against love's high hopes

We are content to watch
The fire in the hearth falter
We know we are dying
But we do nothing
We say nothing
We are content to sit and watch

* * *

Iqbal, we are dying
We have confined ourselves to ourselves
We have become all that is
And we have made all that is become us
We abuse the gift of life
Have lost the gift of love
We have abandoned our trust
And have begun to trust our abandonment
We feel secure in our selfishness
We believe in our helplessness
We accept cowardice with equanimity
We have rejected the possibilities of life

* * *

That prayer is the seed of life we know not
That life is prayer transformed we care not
That every act of a Muslim should be an act of worship
That every act of a Muslim must be an act of worship
Are subjects we would rather not talk about
And a Muslim's very breathing an act of prayer
A thought we would rather not entertain
Sufficient for us the once a day, once a week, prayer
Sufficient for us the decoration of prayer
Sufficient for us the ritual without the spirit
Sufficient for us the prayer with one eye on the clock
And the other eye on God

* * *

Iqbal, it is winter here still
It has been like this ever since you went away
The season is slow in turning
We need the rain, Iqbal
We need the soil, the seed and the sun
We need the will, Iqbal

We need the will to plant the seed
To cultivate the land
To harvest the crop
We need the crop, Iqbal
The drought has lasted too long
We need the sustenance

And then Iqbal, perhaps
We shall be strong once more
To face the storms
Steer an unwavering course
Turn the wide expanse of the sea
And the wider expanse of the sky
The earth, the stars and the deep beyond
To mosques, libraries, laboratories, courts of justice
Strong in knowledge
Stronger in love
Making our every thought, our every act
A searching, a sharing, a striving without end.

Jeremy Cronin (b 1949)

Cronin was born and brought up in Simon's Town, the son of an officer of the South African Navy. He studied at the University of Cape Town and in Paris. He lectured at the University of Cape Town. He was arrested in 1976 and charged and convicted for aiding the ANC, then a banned organization. He spent seven years in various security prisons in Pretoria, including three years among death row prisoners. On his release in 1983 he returned to UCT. After the unbanning of political organizations, he became the Deputy General Secretary of the South African Communist Party. While he was in prison his wife unexpectedly died.

Faraway city, there

Faraway city, there
with salt in its stones,
under its windswept doek,

There in our Cape Town where
they're smashing down homes
of the hungry, labouring people
– will you wait for me, my love?

In that most beautiful,
desolate city of my heart
where if staying on were passive
life wouldn't be what it is.

Not least for those rebuilding
yet again their demolished homes
with bits of plastic, port jackson saplings,
anything to hand – unshakeably

Defiant, frightened, broken,
and unbreakable are the people of our city.

– Will you wait for me, my love?

Visiting room

To admit light,
that's a window's vocation,
or a man to a wife
at this very place
where the wall becomes
for the briefest moments – a window,
shadowed by warders.
A glass plate, its sheer
quiddity, its coldness

forever between our hands.

I saw your mother

I saw your mother
with two guards
through a glass plate
for one quarter hour
on the day that you died.

'Extra visit, special favour'
I was told, and warned
'The visit will be stopped
if politics is discussed.
Verstaan – understand!?'
on the day that you died.

I couldn't place
my arm around her,
around your mother
when she sobbed.

Fifteen minutes up
I was led
back to the workshop.
Your death, my wife,
one crime they managed
not to perpetrate
on the day that you died.

James Fenton (b 1949)

Fenton was born in Lincoln in the United Kingdom and was educated at Oxford. He has worked as a political and literary journalist, and as a war correspondent. His account of the fall of Saigon in Vietnam is well known. He has published a number of collections of poems, including *The Memory of War and Children in Exile* and *Out of Danger*, which won the Whitbread Prize for poetry in 1993. In 1994 he was elected Professor of Poetry at Oxford.

Cambodia

One man shall smile one day and say goodbye.
Two shall be left, two shall be left to die.

One man shall give his best advice.
Three men shall pay the price.

One man shall live, live to regret.
Four men shall meet the debt.

One man shall wake from terror to his bed.
Five men shall be dead.

One man to five. A million men to one.
And still they die. And still the war goes on.

Hinterhof

Stay near to me and I'll stay near to you –
As near as you are dear to me will do,
        Near as the rainbow to the rain,
        The west wind to the windowpane,
As fire to the hearth, as dawn to dew.

Stay true to me and I'll stay true to you –
As true as you are new to me will do,
        New as the rainbow in the spray,
        Utterly new in every way,
New in the way that what you say is true.

Stay near to me, stay true to me. I'll stay
As near, as true to you as heart could pray.
        Heart never hoped that one might be
        Half of the things you are to me –
The dawn, the fire, the rainbow and the day.

Nigel Fogg (b 1949)

Fogg was born in Johannesburg, and went to school in Grahamstown. After
interrupting his university fine-arts studies, he earned a BA degree in African
Politics and African Development Administration. He has worked as a leather-
craftsperson and a photographer, spending four years as curator of photographs
at the South African National Gallery. In 1986 he left South Africa, and now lives
in south-west France, where he runs a business making specialist camera bags.

Magnolia Clinic

On entering
I threw my false voice at you
and yours came back
across the sterilized distance.

Smothered in a world of white
you were connected
by a long plastic tube
to a hole in the wall
labelled 'Life'.

There were the usual questions
and your usual lies

and while mother continued
I turned to face the sets of eyes
watching the Englishman's son.
I greeted them: 'Hullo'
which was neither here nor there.

Through the window
there was a tree with leaves
and a bird,
and though late
traces of a long sun
unretreated among the park.

One day father
I suppose I shall turn
from the window
and find you withdrawn
into your hole in the wall
and turn again
to discover the bird gone
and the sun retreated
and mother and I shall leave
empty-lunged
walking
between shadow and shade
always.

Musaemura Zimunya (b 1949)

Zimunya was born in Mutare (then Umtali) in Zimbabwe (then Rhodesia). In 1975 he was imprisoned, following a student demonstration. He went into exile, and studied at the University of Kent. He returned to independent Zimbabwe to teach in the Department of English at the University of Zimbabwe.

Cattle in the rain

Nothing has no end,
it is true.
This rain used to soak us in the pastures
and the cattle would not stop to graze,
they would not be driven to the kraal,

it made me cry and curse sometimes
and I used to wish I was born for the skirt.
Just imagine penetrating the wet bush
almost doubled up
with a heavy smelling coned-up jute sack
as a raincoat,
pebbles of water pounding on the head,
very irritating, too.
Sometimes an angry wasp disturbed by the foregoing cows
stabbed you on the cursing lips
and in the frantic stampede,
wet thorns snapped at random in your benumbed feet.

And the rain does not cease
and the cows just go on.

Come to the kraal –
This ox, called Gatooma,
stands still before the rest,
his ghost of silent disapproval shattering your mind,
listening, listening to nothing at all,
and I knew then that I had to call for help.
But people at home in warm huts
could hardly hear me through the maddening rain.
This ox, tail high,
in two sniffs and a cajole,
all meant to humiliate
would crash through the thin bush
leaving me running weakly
sobbing at each step
a bone of anger blocking my breath,
chugging after the rhythmic hooves hammering the earth.
And still it rained
and the cows went skelter
and the rain swept the salty tears
and watery mucus into my lips.

Joy Lowe is a South African missionary who, with her husband, worked for years at Chikore Mission (Eastern Highlands) before being deported by the Rhodesian Front government. The Lowes are close friends of the poet.

The reason

To Joy Lowe

In my letter
I feared the loss of love
inside me.
Apologies that it shocked you
I was only being frank.
Every day you see all these men –
prisoners –
misery playing a dead show
in their countenances
laughing, unconscious of
the negativeness their voices betray;
some of them too innocent to kill a louse
others too old to know whether they are dead
or alive.
The backs of these old men bled,
perhaps they gave food to guerrilla fighters.
I was shown one back; an incomprehensible
tattoo of sjambok tracks showing pink,
and this man will be here for five years.
A grandad from the backwoods,
he knows not what Rhodesia is,
what Zimbabwe is or what this war is all about!

Conscience lambasts you
like a gust of the August wind and
disappears like a wisp of cigar smoke
questions unanswered block your thinking
frustration fumes and fumes.

Now where is the room
for love?

Amelia Blossom House (b 1940s)

House (known also by her married name Pegram) was born in Wynberg near Cape Town. She was educated at the Hewat Teacher Training College and the University of Cape Town. After teaching in Cape Town for seven years, she went to London, where she taught and studied drama at the Guildhall School of Music and Drama. In 1972 she moved to the United States, and obtained an MA degree from the University of Louisville, Kentucky, where she currently teaches. She has published *Deliverance: Poems for South Africa* and *Our Sun Will Rise*.

I will still sing

It is my celebration
I will drum my drum
I will sing my song
I will dance my dance
I do not need your anemic hands
brought together in pale applause
I do not need your
'You are such musical people'
toothy smile
It is my celebration
You wonder what I have to celebrate
What does the drum tell me
If you must speculate
Watch Out
One day as you throw your head back
As you gather your hearty laughter
I will change my dance
I will still sing
The drum will scream
Celebration.

Mavis Smallberg (b 1940s)

Smallberg was born in South Africa. She wrote this poem in response to an article by Susan Sussens in the *Weekend Argus* of 25 August 1986. (Note that 'Gilly' was a misprint in the newspaper; the boy's name was 'Willy Nyathele'.) Mavis Smallberg teaches in Cape Town.

A small boy

For Gilly Nyathele, aged twelve

First the face, and then
the caption caught my eye:
    Small Boy Seen As
    Threat to State Security

The face is oval
the cheekbones high
the mouth a generous curve
and then,
those eyes!
The eyes are almond-shaped
with wrinkles underneath;
those eyes show largely white;
the expression in those
serious sullen eyes
is a danger to the State!

A small boy should not have
such eyes;
eyes which glower, two black coals
smouldering on the page;
eyes which cannot seem to smile;
eyes unfathomable
filled with hate, or tinged
with fear?
eyes which look as if they've
never known a tear
a small boy should not have
such eyes

A small boy should not be
detained.
A small boy should not be
in jail.
Not once,
not thrice,
not four times in a row!
A small boy should not be
shut into a cell

so that he can break
a small boy should not be
a danger to the State!

And yet
that small boy knows the slogans
knows he has to fight
a system which pays his mother
sixty rands per month.
The small boy
fights against grown men who
pose as 'vigilantes'.
The small boy
frowns when comrades drink
getting drunk inside shebeens.
The small boy
with a hundred others who call
themselves 'the fourteens'
'run the place' – Tumehole,
a township in Free State.
This small boy
just released from
Heilbron prison in Parys

But right now
the small boy only wants
'to eat and eat and eat'
he fidgets in his chair and says:
'white children sit in chairs
like these'.
The small boy talks about
democracy
and says his brushes with the
state has only made him 'stubborn'.
This small boy,
this Gilly Nyathele,
who with his three brothers
live on salt and porridge
and who, together with his sister,
often hungry goes to sleep.
This small boy knows his fate
and wants his country
free

Ah, woe betide our fate
that such
a small boy
is a danger to the State!

Grace Nichols (b 1950)

Nichols was born in Guyana, educated at the University of Guyana, and moved
to live in the United Kingdom in 1977. Among her collections of poems are *i is a
long memoried woman* (which won the Commonwealth Prize for Poetry in 1983)
and *The Fat Black Woman's Poems*. See also the other Caribbean writers in this
collection, for instance Derek Walcott (p. 129), James Berry (p. 102), John Agard
(p. 203), Linton Kwesi Johnson (p. 228), and Heather Royes (p. 246). Lemn Sissay
(p. 268) and Benjamin Zephaniah (p. 241), born in the United Kingdom, also
have West Indian origins.

Compare the first poem with Jennifer Davids's 'Poem for my mother' (p. 189)
and the second poem with Sylvia Plath's 'You're' (p. 138).

Praise song for my mother

You were
water to me
deep and bold and fathoming

You were
moon's eye to me
pull and grained and mantling

You were
sunrise to me
rise and warm and streaming

You were
the fishes red gill to me
the flame tree's spread to me
the crab's leg/the fried plantain smell
                    replenishing replenishing

Go to your wide futures, you said

In my name

Heavy with child

belly
an arc
of black moon

I squat over
dry plantain leaves

and command the earth
to receive you

in my name
in my blood

to receive you
my curled bean

my tainted
perfect child

       my bastard fruit
       my seedling
       my sea grape
       my strange mulatto
       my little bloodling

Let the snake slipping in deep grass
be dumb before you

Let the centipede writhe and shrivel
in its tracks

Let the evil one strangle on his own tongue
even as he sets his eyes upon you

For with my blood
I've cleansed you
and with my tears
I've pooled the river Niger

now my sweet one it is for you to swim

Ingrid de Kok (b 1951)

De Kok was brought up in Stilfontein, a small mining town in what was then the western Transvaal. She was educated at the Universities of the Witwatersrand and Cape Town, as well as at Queens' University in Canada. She has had one collection of her poems published, *Familiar Ground*. She is Director of Extra-Mural Studies at the University of Cape Town.

Small passing

For a woman whose baby died stillborn, and who was told by a man to stop mourning, 'because the trials and horrors suffered daily by black women in this country are more significant than the loss of one white child'.

1

In this country you may not
suffer the death of your stillborn,
remember the last push into shadow and silence,
the useless wires and cords on your stomach,
the nurse's face, the walls, the afterbirth in a basin.
Do not touch your breasts
still full of purpose.
Do not circle the house,
pack, unpack the small clothes.
Do not lie awake at night hearing
the doctor say 'It was just as well'
and 'You can have another.'
In this country you may not
mourn small passings.

See: the newspaper boy in the rain
will sleep tonight in a doorway.
The woman in the busline
may next month be on a train
to a place not her own.
The baby in the backyard now
will be sent to a tired aunt,
grow chubby, then lean,
return a stranger.
Mandela's daughter tried to find her father
through the glass. She thought they'd let her touch him.
And this woman's hands are so heavy when she dusts

the photographs of other children
they fall to the floor and break.
Clumsy woman, she moves so slowly
as if in a funeral rite.

On the pavements the nannies meet.
These are legal gatherings.
They talk about everything, about home,
while the children play among them,
their skins like litmus, their bonnets clean.

2

Small wrist in the grave.
Baby no one carried live
between houses, among trees.
Child shot running,
stones in his pocket,
boy's swollen stomach
full of hungry air.
Girls carrying babies
not much smaller than themselves.
Erosion. Soil washed down to the sea.

3

I think these mothers dream
headstones of the unborn.
Their mourning rises like a wall
no vine will cling to.
They will not tell you your suffering is white.
They will not say it is just as well.
They will not compete for the ashes of infants.
I think they may say to you:
Come with us to the place of mothers.
We will stroke your flat empty belly,
let you weep with us in the dark,
and arm you with one of our babies
to carry home on your back.

Safe delivery

for Jonah Lewis

I claim kin, giddy newborn sprite
since you were conceived after the close dancing
of your begetters and deliverers
in my living room late one August night.

Your birth was a constricting band
denying you familiar dark circulation;
then a rush of air, gush of light
splashed you through the net of your mother,

slippery into your own body
into your own nine lives
and into the amateur hands
of your parent midwives:

one hand attached to a phone,
one holding a do-it-yourself book,
a third adjusting the bed and a fourth
basketting your pulsing head.

Born in a caul, coughed out of the belly
of the whale, wide-eyed, quivery.
Now blossoming into family flesh.
I wish you well in your human livery.

Moira Lovell (b 1951)

Lovell was born in Zimbabwe, and moved to South Africa in 1976. She now lives
and teaches in KwaZulu-Natal. She has had one volume of poems published,
Out of the Mist. She has written a number of stage and radio plays.

Suburban intruder

Secure in our multi-walls
With manicured grass beyond,
We anticipate some buzzers and crawlers
And despatch them cleanly
Under spotlights of spray.

But we shake to encounter
A spiky black rat
Balancing on the bath-tub
Eating the soap 'for a more beautiful you'.

Lathering at the whiskers
It lunges at a net curtain
And nails its way up
To measure its tail against the drop.
A final swing throws it into the night.

We observe the invisible footprints
Patterning the gloss of the bath ...
And ring the Rat-Ex man.

'Eating the soap, you say?
Ja, that'd be a sewer rat.
Come up through the loo.
Good job you weren't on it, hey?'
And he grins his yellow teeth.

Now, in the middle of the night,
When the call comes, we seldom obey,
Being a little threatened
Within our walls.

Repossession

It's a movie filmed
By the same old Director
And I'm the leading lady
Not acting an anonymous
White madam meandering
In four o'clock sunlight
Down a filigree-labelled lane
In the Victorian labyrinth
Of central town
Where quite suddenly
A trio of Afro-
Gucci Carduccis
Are choking my passage
Shoving my voice
Down my throat

Bullying my shoulder
For the bag that swings
Heavily with my identity;
They trophy it away
And I am left falling
In slow motion
Among flimsy buildings
That collapse with me
In a vertical pan.

Mike Nicol (b 1951)

Nicol was born in Cape Town, where he now works as a journalist. He has published a number of novels, two collections of verse, and an account of the *Drum* writers of the 1950s (see Stan Motjuwadi, p. 130).
    This poem was included in a collection of poems published in 1978.

New men

I suppose revolutions have all been the same:
Matters reach the point of no return,
The powers that be continue their polities
Of steel suppression, so all hell breaks loose.
Blood is called for and the masses go
Pounding through city streets, stoning, looting,
And burning until the bastille is breached
And the new regime sits solemnly in government.

I have some truck with revolutions, holding
That if the present order's got out of hand
The ballot box is useless which leaves no choice
But bloody insurrection. Take France. The snotty
Aristocracy got all they asked for. You can't
Keep the people down, I say, they'll up and at you
One day. Injustice schools long memories
That balance the past with a precise revenge.

Revolution, though, is far too strong a word.
It's never really that. I'll wager
In some French vineyard a peasant
Went about his daily labour under a warm sun
While his comrades trundled the snivelling nobility

To the guillotine. And in Petrograd, I've read,
Most people didn't know the revolt was on.
The trams were running, the theatres crowded,

Chaliapin sang at the Opera, the fashionable
Ate in the best restaurants. The Red Guards
Were just as diffident: walked in the gutters,
Steered clear of the smart quarter. So
Rebellion doesn't always mean thousands are killed:
The waves of unrest mightn't touch the farmer
Ploughing a field, or the ladies at bookclub
In a peaceful suburb. Of course,

It's worse in towns, fear keeps doors locked
And windows barred, guns are as common as
Walkingsticks, people do get killed, refugees
Take off. It's difficult to tell just when
Revolutions start. The odd riot strikes a match
And before long it's flared in major centres.
The June days were like that: the death-toll mounted
Quickly, and although I sympathised, believing added

Misery must produce resistance, the mood was anti-white.
Since then feelings haven't changed, but the situation's
Ripe and the bourgeois are lulled. Today police
In camouflage gear are common sights, and when
TV news shows rioting in some dismal township,
Or bulldozers at work on someone's home
It doesn't mean that much in an evening lounge
Where the family are drinking tea and knitting.

These things are happening all around us: men
Have been machine-gunned in our streets. Funerals
Broken-up, houses raided, people battered
By riot-squads. Yet like the peasant farmer or
Ivanovich Chaliapin, I must turn to mundane affairs,
But end with a persistent thought: there
Is widespread despair, yet hard ground is breaking
And will soon set afoot a new man in our cities.

Kelwyn Sole (b 1951)

Sole was born in Johannesburg, was educated at the Universities of the
Witwatersrand and London, and has worked in Namibia and Botswana. He now
teaches English at the University of Cape Town. He has had two collections of
poems published, *The Blood of Our Silence* and *Projections in the Past Tense*.

In 1984 the people of Magopa (or Mogopa) were forcibly removed from their
land and placed against their wishes in Pachsdraai. The Nkomati Accord was a
non-aggression pact between Mozambique and South Africa forced on President
Samora Machel in 1984.

My countrymen

As our treacherous land spins now
away from the sun, and a carpet of stars
descends on the cold floor
of winter

we, separately, yawn
brush our teeth with the defence budget
and go to bed without each other –
the Magopa patriarch flung at Pachsdraai
a clod of crumbled soil;
the cleaner who'll climb the skyscraper night
now cooks her husband's supper
already sick with tiredness

and old and powerful men
sucking their thumbs in sleep, one hand curled
round the cuddlesome security of the Nkomati Accord,
faces blissful

and the rest of us

the many lessons we haven't learnt
the courageous stands we never took
the synapse between pain and knowledge
of ourselves, our nerve ends bathed
in acetylcholine and history
where fate plays roulette with our skin
(but we daren't call it russian)

my countrymen

of the homespun hopeful visions
we wear as underwear this season

our night has come again

Tiny victories

Sometimes tiny victories
for the white working class.
Our Kentucky Fried Chicken in Kitchener
Avenue won a hugely glaucous cup
moersa ugly
for best outlet of the month.
So they promoted the black manager
and gave us a white boy sprouting pimples
gap-toothed and stupid, in his place.

Linton Kwesi Johnson (b 1952)

Johnson was born in Jamaica, and moved to the United Kingdom at the age of
eleven. He went to school in London and studied sociology at the University of
London. He joined the Black Panthers, formed a group of poets and drummers
called Rasta Love, and launched his own record label, LKJ. He coined the phrase
'dub poetry' for the musical idiom of black British poetry closely associated
with the Caribbean and with reggae. Four collections of his poems have been
published, and a number of albums released. In 1985 he was made an Associate
Fellow of Warwick University, and in 1987 an Honorary Fellow of Wolver-
hampton Polytechnic.

Mekkin histri

now tell mi someting
mistah govahment man
tell mi someting

how lang yu really feel
yu coulda keep wi andah heel
wen di trute done reveal
bout how yu grab an steal
bout how yu mek yu crooked deal
mek yu crooked deal?

well doun in Soutall
where Peach did get fall
di Asians dem faam-up a human wall
gense di fashist an dem police sheil
an dem show dat di Asians gat plenty zeal
      gat plenty zeal
      gat plenty zeal

it is noh mistri
wi mekkin histri
it is noh mistri
wi winnin victri

now tell mi someting
mistah police spokesman
tell mi someting

how lang yu really tink
wi woulda tek yu batn lick
yu jackboot kick
yu dutty bag a tricks
an yu racist pallyticks
yu racist pallyticks?

well doun in Bristal
dey ad noh pistal
but dem chaste di babylan away
man yu shoulda si yu babylan
how dem really run away
yu shoulda si yu babylan dem dig-up dat day
      dig-up dat day
      dig-up dat day

it is noh mistri
wi mekkin histri
it is noh mistri
wi winnin victri

now tell mi someting
mistah ritewing man
tell mi someting

how lang yu really feel
wi woulda grovel an squeal

wen soh much murdah canceal
wen wi woun cyaan heal
wen wi feel di way wi feel
feel di way wi feel?

well dere woz Toxteth
an dere woz Moss Side
an a lat a addah places
whey di police ad to hide
well dare woz Brixtan
an dere woz Chapeltoun
an a lat a addah place dat woz burnt to di groun
                                burnt to di groun
                                burnt to di groun

it is noh mistri
wi mekkin histri
it is noh mistri
wi winnin victri

Farouk Asvat (b 1952)

Asvat was brought up in Johannesburg. He was listed as a banned person for five years in the 1970s. He is a medical doctor.

See the note that precedes Christopher van Wyk's poem 'In detention' (p. 240). 'SBs' refers to the Special (Political) Branch of the South African Police under the National Party government.

Possibilities for a man hunted by SBs

There's one of two possibilities
Either they find you or they don't
If they don't it's ok
But if they find you
There's one of two possibilities
Either they let you go or they ban you
If they let you go it's ok
But if they ban you
There's one of two possibilities
Either you break your ban or you don't

If you don't it's ok
But if you break your ban
There's one of two possibilities
Either they find out or they don't
If they don't it's ok
But if they find out
There's one of two possibilities
Either they find you guilty or notguilty
If they find you notguilty it's ok
But if they find you guilty
There's one of two possibilities
Either they suspend your sentence or they jail you
If they suspend your sentence it's ok
But if they jail you
There's one of two possibilities
Either they release you
Or you fall from the tenth floor

Chenjerai Hove (b 1954)

Hove was born in Mazvihwa in Zimbabwe. He was educated at the University of
Rhodesia, and has been writer-in-residence at the University of Zimbabwe. He
has published several collections of poems, a collection of short pieces titled
Shebeen Tales, and three novels, *Bones* (which won the 1989 Noma Award for
Publishing in Africa), *Shadows,* and *Ancestors.*

A war-torn wife

This war!
I am tired
of a husband who never sleeps
guarding the home or on call-up,
Never sleeping!

Maybe inside him he says
'I am tired of a wife
who never dies
so I could stop guarding.'

How does this next poem relate to Charles Mungoshi's 'If you don't stay bitter for too long' (p. 193)?

You will forget

If you stay in comfort too long
you will not know
the weight of a water pot
on the bald head of the village woman

You will forget
the weight of three bundles of thatch grass
on the sinewy neck of the woman
whose baby cries on her back
for a blade of grass in its eyes

Sure, if you stay in comfort too long
you will not know the pain
of child birth without a nurse in white

You will forget
the thirst, the cracked dusty lips
of the woman in the valley
on her way to the headman who isn't there

You will forget
the pouring pain of a thorn prick
with a load on the head.
If you stay in comfort too long

You will forget
the wailing in the valley
of women losing a husband in the mines.

You will forget
the rough handshake of coarse palms
full of teary sorrow at the funeral.

If you stay in comfort too long
You will not hear
the shrieky voice of old warriors sing
the songs of fresh stored battlefields.

You will forget
the unfeeling bare feet
gripping the warm soil turned by the plough

You will forget
the voice of the season talking to the oxen.

Stephen Watson (b 1954)

Watson was born and educated in Cape Town. He has published a book of
literary essays and four volumes of poems, including *Return of the Moon* and
Presence of the Earth. He teaches in the English Department at the University
of Cape Town.

Commonplaces

It had been commonplace enough, for his time and place.
He'd met her back in Durban, when she was still in school.
Within a month they'd set up house, her parents disowning her.
She'd leave their bed, a Berea flat, for one last year in school;
he for his job, as shipping clerk, on Durban's waterfront.

Nor was it that unusual when one year to the day,
their young romance already old, she ran off with his best friend.
Six, seven years have passed since then. She's long since
left that friend as well. She never finished school.

But those were years he'd been obsessed with her,
boring all his Cape Town friends with her betrayal, her perfidy,
but writing to her all the same, long after he'd left Durban,
talking always of her, even taking correspondence courses
so he'd be forced to study, to stay at home each evening,
so he'd always be there on the off-chance she might phone.

It takes four years, even five – so the textbooks say –
to get over a bad jilting. So none of this surprised us much –
nothing like the day he mentioned, quite in passing,
he'd lost all contact with her, hadn't heard a word in months.

Apparently, she'd moved again; this time who knows where.
Perhaps, he told us, he'd still bump into her, should he
go back to Durban. But probably not – at least not now.

After all, it was so long ago, and he'd heard she'd started drinking.
He'd nothing left to say to her, had outgrown her in every way.

'She's history now,' he said, 'something over. Of the past.'
She was no more, by now, than one phrase among the many,
the plain and final phrases, all but painless, that consign
lives to the great rubbish-heap of anyone's past loves, dead hates.

She was history now, he told us, who heard him out once more,
hearing, as he fell silent, as if we'd never heard it all before,
the cruelty in the commonplace – all that's left, that appals
in these scandals of the everyday, tortures of the ordinary.

Carol Ann Duffy (b 1955)

Duffy was born in Glasgow, grew up in Staffordshire, attended university in
Liverpool, and now lives and works in London. She has published a number of
collections of poems, including *Standing Female Nude* and *Selling Manhattan*.
Her 1993 collection *Mean Time* won the Whitbread Award for poetry.

Foreign

Imagine living in a strange, dark city for twenty years.
There are some dismal dwellings on the east side
and one of them is yours. On the landing, you hear
your foreign accent echo down the stairs. You think
in a language of your own and talk in theirs.

Then you are writing home. The voice in your head
recites the letter in a local dialect; behind that
is the sound of your mother singing to you,
all that time ago, and now you do not know
why your eyes are watering and what's the word for this.

You use the public transport. Work. Sleep. Imagine one night
you saw a name for yourself sprayed in red
against a brick wall. A hate name. Red like blood.
It is snowing on the streets, under the neon lights,
as if this place were coming to bits before your eyes.

And in the delicatessen, from time to time, the coins
in your palm will not translate. Inarticulate,

because this is not home, you point at fruit. Imagine
that one of you says *Me not know what these people mean.*
It like they only go to bed and dream. Imagine that.

In the next poem the names 'Brady and Hindley' refer to notorious child-
murderers in the 1960s.

In Mrs Tilscher's class

You could travel up the Blue Nile
with your finger, tracing the route
while Mrs Tilscher chanted the scenery.
Tana. Ethiopia. Khartoum. Aswân.
That for an hour, then a skittle of milk
and the chalky Pyramids rubbed into dust.
A window opened with a long pole.
The laugh of a bell swung by a running child.

This was better than home. Enthralling books.
The classroom glowed like a sweetshop.
Sugar paper. Coloured shapes. Brady and Hindley
faded, like the faint, uneasy smudge of a mistake.
Mrs Tilscher loved you. Some mornings, you found
she'd left a good gold star by your name.
The scent of a pencil slowly, carefully, shaved.
A xylophone's nonsense heard from another form.

Over the Easter term, the inky tadpoles changed
from commas into exclamation marks. Three frogs
hopped in the playground, freed by a dunce,
followed by a line of kids, jumping and croaking
away from the lunch queue. A rough boy
told you how you were born. You kicked him, but stared
at your parents, appalled, when you got back home.

That feverish July, the air tasted of electricity.
A tangible alarm made you always untidy, hot,
fractious under the heavy, sexy sky. You asked her
how you were born and Mrs Tilscher smiled,
then turned away. Reports were handed out.
You ran through the gates, impatient to be grown,
as the sky split open into a thunderstorm.

Fhazel Johennesse (b 1956)

Johennesse was born in Johannesburg. He was the co-editor of *Wietie* literary magazine in the eighties. His collection of poems is called *The Rainmaker*.

the night train

there is no comfort here
in this third class coach
on this green resisting seat
i twitch and glance around –
there are few too few travellers
on the night train
crossing my legs and flicking
my cigarette i turn to stare
through the window
into the darkness outside
(or is it my reflection i stare at)
and glance impatiently at the wrong
stations we stop at
out
i must get out of here soon
for in this coach there is a smell
which haunts me
not the smell of stale man but
the whispering nagging smell of fear

the nightwatchman

the fire looks warm from here
and a red reflection diffuses and
glows across his face
he sits quite still a grey overcoat
drawn taut over his back
then i see his fingers move agitate
and briefly a flicker of firelight
paints a smile on his face and then
melts it again
i watch his fingers they slowly
slip across the scalloped edge

of the knobkerrie
and suddenly i know

i know that he waits for the
cracking of skulls and the
breaking of bones

a young man's thoughts before june the 16th

tomorrow i travel on a road
that winds to the top of the hill
i take with me only the sweet
memories of my youth
my heart aches for my mother
for friday nights with friends
around a table with the broad belch of beer
i ask only for a sad song
sung by a woman with downturned eyes
and strummed by an old man with
a broken brow
o sing my sad song sing for me
for my sunset is drenched with red

Karen Press (b 1956)

Press was born and lives in Cape Town. She has run her own small publishing
house, Buchu Books. Three volumes of her poems have appeared.

When your child is born, mother

When your child is born, mother
place a songbird at your nipple
and fix the child's mouth to the rationed tap.
Bitter water its comfort, dust of the street its cradle.

When your child is born, mother
give your heart to a piece of land,
and when the child goes out
to fight, sing out across the land
and when they bring the body back
clutch the land to your breast, and build your house there.

When your child is born, mother
pour your love into a clay pot,
bury it in a corner of the house.
If the future comes, there will be wine for the feast.
If the future does not come, there will be water for a small grave.

Do not sit waiting over the supper pot;
you must unlearn the old lessons
your mother taught you: look at your children,
mothers, look at your children, these small stones
building a road through the country,
these graves like footsteps towards the harvest.

Clever man

Clever man, hey, you're really impressive!
Come tell me some more about these heavy things.
Explain again about labour relations, the economics
of exploitation, the theory of surplus value.
Then while I'm still reeling under the weight
of your thoughts, tell me
what that woman's doing on her hands and knees
on the kitchen floor.
Oh – she's your wife.

Now tell me about the psychology of the oppressed.
Explain how people internalise the oppressor's vision.
Give me an example of negative self-image induced
by exposure to a combination of material and ideological forces
that leave one no choice but to believe one's oppression is
justified. Then quickly,
before my note-taking hand seizes up with cramp, tell me
why your wife standing making your supper
answers into her chest as you slap her backside
and ask 'How's things old girl? No complaints?'
– 'Everything's fine.'

Not forgetting

summer's coming, despite everything,
sit on the beach and think of your brother
in prison, remember your sister in the graveyard

spread out your towel and imagine
one thin line of sky painted behind bars and walls
cold as a black coffin, buy an ice-cream
for your brother, taste it with your sister's tongue
ride a wave for each of them, you must
live three times over now, not forgetting yourself

Christopher van Wyk (b 1957)

Van Wyk was born in Newclare in Johannesburg, and matriculated from
Riverlea High School. He has been an educational researcher. With Fhazel
Johennesse (see p. 236) he edited the literary journal *Wietie*, and he was also the
editor of *Staffrider* literary magazine. He won the Olive Schreiner Prize for his
collection of poems *It Is Time To Go Home*.

Injustice

Me, I cry easily if you're hurt
and I would've carried the crosses
of both the murderer
and the thief
if they'd've let me
and I'd've lived then.

I grasp helplessly at cigarettes
during riots
and burn my fingers
hoping.

My nose has never sniffed teargas
but I weep all the same
and my heart hurts
aching from buckshot.

My dreams these days are policed
by a million eyes
that baton-charge my sleep
and frog-march me into a
shaken morning.

I can't get used to injustice.
I can't smile no matter what.

I'll never get used to nightmares
but often I dream of freedom.

During the apartheid years many deaths occurred while people were detained by the police (Steve Biko was the forty-sixth in 1977). The official reasons given for these deaths were often as derisory as they were grotesque. For instance, Ahmed Timol (d 1971) 'fell from a tenth floor window' at Johannesburg Security Police headquarters, Imam Abdullah Haron (d 1969) 'slipped down the stairs', no explanation being given for the twenty seven bruises found on his body, and Solomon Modipane (d 1969) 'slipped on a piece of soap and fatally injured himself'.

In detention

He fell from the ninth floor
He hanged himself
He slipped on a piece of soap while washing
He hanged himself
He slipped on a piece of soap while washing
He fell from the ninth floor
He hanged himself while washing
He slipped from the ninth floor
He hung from the ninth floor
He slipped on the ninth floor while washing
He fell from a piece of soap while slipping
He hung from the ninth floor
He washed from the ninth floor while slipping
He hung from a piece of soap while washing

A 'hippo' was an armoured vehicle used by the police.

A riot policeman

The sun has gone down
with the last doused flame.
Tonight's last bullet
has singed the day's last victim
an hour ago.
It is time to go home.

The hippo crawls
in a desultory air of triumph
through, around fluttering
shirts and shoes full of death.
Teargas is simmering.
Tears have been dried by heat
or cooled by death.
Buckshot fills the space
between the maimed and the mourners.
It is time to go home.

A black man surrenders
a stolen bottle of brandy
scurries away with his life
in his hands.
The policeman rests the oasis
on his lips
wipes his mouth on a camouflaged
cuff.
It is time to go home.

Tonight he'll shed his uniform.
Put on his pyjamas.
Play with his children.
Make love to his wife.
Tomorrow is pay-day.
But it is time to go home now,
It is time to go home.

Benjamin Zephaniah (b 1958)

Zephaniah was born in Birmingham in the United Kingdom, spending some of
his childhood in Jamaica. His early teens were spent in various approved schools
and in prison. He became a Rastafarian, and a well-known performance dub
poet. He has written poems, plays, film-scripts, and worked as an actor and
recording artist. He has performed his work in Zimbabwe and in South Africa.

According to my mood

i have poetic licence, i WriTe thE
    way i waNt.
i drop my full stops where i
    like …

MY CAPITAL LeteRs go where i
liKE.
i order from MY PeN, i verse the
    way i like (i do my spelling write)
According to My MOod.
i HAve poetic licence.
i put my commers where i like,,((()).
(((my brackets are write((
I REPEAT WHen i likE.
i can't go rong,
i look and i.c.
It's rite.
i REpeat when i liKE. i have
poetic licence!
don't question me????

Gcina Mhlophe (b 1959)

Mhlophe was born in Hammarsdale, and grew up in the Eastern Cape.
She is South Africa's foremost story-teller, with a number of published
children's books. She is also a playwright (*Have You Seen Zandile?* has
played internationally), poet, and short story writer.

Sometimes when it rains

Sometimes when it rains
I smile to myself
And think of times when as a child
I'd sit by myself
And wonder why people need clothes

Sometimes when it rains
I think of times
when I'd run into the rain
Shouting 'Nkce – nkce mlanjana
When will I grow?
I'll grow up tomorrow!'

Sometimes when it rains
I think of times
When I watched goats

running so fast from the rain
While sheep seemed to enjoy it

Sometimes when it rains
I think of times
When we had to undress
Carry the small bundles of uniforms and books
On our heads
And cross the river after school

Sometimes when it rains
I remember times
When it would rain hard for hours
And fill our drum
so we didn't have to fetch water
From the river for a day or two

Sometimes when it rains
Rains for many hours without break
I think of people
who have nowhere to go
No home of their own
And no food to eat
Only rain water to drink

Sometimes when it rains
Rains for days without break
I think of mothers
Who give birth in squatter camps
Under plastic shelters
At the mercy of cold angry winds

Sometimes when it rains
I think of 'illegal' job seekers
in big cities
Dodging police vans in the rain
Hoping for darkness to come
So they can find some wet corner to hide in

Sometimes when it rains
Rains so hard hail joins in
I think of life prisoners
in all the jails of the world

and wonder if they still love
To see the rainbow at the end of the rain

Sometimes when it rains
With hail stones biting the grass
I can't help thinking they look like teeth
Many teeth of smiling friends
Then I wish that everyone else
Had something to smile about.

The dancer

Mama,
they tell me you were a dancer
they tell me you had long
beautiful legs to carry your graceful body
they tell me you were a dancer

Mama,
they tell me you sang beautiful solos
they tell me you closed your eyes
always when the feeling of the song
was right, and lifted your face up to the sky
they tell me you were an enchanting dancer

Mama,
they tell me you were always so gentle
they talk of a willow tree
swaying lovingly over clear running water
in early Spring when they talk of you
they tell me you were a slow dancer

Mama,
they tell me you were a wedding dancer
they tell me you smiled and closed your eyes
your arms curving outward just a little
and your feet shuffling in the sand;
tshi tshi tsitshitshitha, tshitshi tshitshitshitha
o hee! how I wish I was there to see you
they tell me you were a pleasure to watch

Mama
they tell me I am a dancer too

but I don't know…
I don't know for sure what a wedding dancer is
there are no more weddings
but many, many funerals
where we sing and dance
running fast with the coffin
of a would-be bride or would-be groom
strange smiles have replaced our tears
our eyes are full of vengeance, Mama

Dear, dear Mama,
they tell me I am a funeral dancer.

Ben Okri (b 1959)

Okri was born in Nigeria, and lives in the United Kingdom. He won the Booker
Prize in 1991 for his novel *The Famished Road*. Several other novels have followed.
His poems are collected in *An African Elegy*.

You walked gently towards me

You walked gently towards me
In the evening light
And brought silence with you
Which fell off when
I touched your shoulder
And felt the rain on it.

We went through the city
Up the roaring streets
Full of many lights
And we sought a place
To be alone
And found none.

The evening was merciful
On your smile.
Your laughter touched
The hungry ghosts
Of passing years.

You moved smoothly
On the waters
Your shadow sounded of silk
You led me to places
Full of mellow darkness
Secret coves where they
Didn't let us in
And under the rain
You bid me kiss you with
Your silent and uncertain eyes.

We walked home
And the rain laughed around us
With its insistent benediction
And your hair was strung with
        Diadems
Your face with glittering dreams
And my eyes were wet
        With your luminous spirited joy.

Heather Royes (b 1950s)

Royes was born in Jamaica, and graduated from the University of the West Indies, followed by postgraduate studies abroad. She works for the Jamaican government, in communications.

The experience of Theophilus Jones in the next poem is clearly extraordinary. Or is it? Something far more extraordinary happened to the legendary Greek character Icarus (see W H Auden's 'Musée des Beaux Arts' (p. 63)).

Theophilus Jones walks naked down King Street

On Monday, October 18th,
Theophilus Jones took off
his asphalt-black, rag-tag pants
and walked naked down King Street.
It was a holiday –
and only a few people saw
his triumphant march,
his muscular, bearded-brown body,
his genitals flapping in front.

Theophilus Jones had wanted
to do this for a long time.

At Tower and King, three carwash boys
shouting 'Madman!', followed him to Harbour Street,
but seeing his indifference, turned
and dribbled back up the road.
Down on the Ferry Pier, a handful of people
waiting for the boat, stared out to sea
but did not see
Theophilus enter the water.
He walked out as far as possible,
then began to swim, strongly and calmly,
into the middle of the harbour.
Eventually, way out in the deep,
he stopped,
floated for a while, enjoying the sun,
watched a plane take off from the green-rimmed palisades,
and then, letting himself go,
allowed the water
to swallow him up.

Theophilus Jones went down
slowly,
slowly his bent legs, slowly
his arms above his head,
slowly his locksed hair,
slowly.
Until nothing could be seen of him.

Some orange-peel, an old tin-can
and a sea-saturated cigarette box
floated over his demise,
while near by,
a kingfisher – scavenging for sprats
on a low current – veered down
and landed,
in a spray of sunlit water.

Magoleng wa Selepe (b 1950s)

This South African poem is quite frequently anthologized, but no information about the poet is available.

My name
Nomgqibelo Ncamisile Mnqhibisa

Look what they have done to my name…
the wonderful name of my great-great-grandmothers
Nomgqibelo Ncamisile Mnqhibisa

The burly bureaucrat was surprised.
What he heard was music to his ears
'Wat is daai, sê nou weer?'
'I am from Chief Daluxolo Velayigodle of emaMpondweni
And my name is *Nomgqibelo Ncamisile Mnqhibisa.*'

Messia, help me!
My name is so simple
and yet so meaningful,
but to this man it is trash…

He gives me a name
Convenient enough to answer his whim:
I end up being
Maria…
I…
Nomgqibelo Ncamisile Mnqhibisa.

Amryl Johnson (b c 1960)

Johnson was born in Trinidad, and was brought up by her grandmother until the age of eleven, when she joined her parents in the United Kingdom. She went to school in London, and took a degree at the University of Kent. She has spent several blocks of time back in the Caribbean.

Granny in de market place

Yuh fish fresh?

Woman, why yuh holdin' meh fish up tuh yuh nose?
De fish fresh. Ah say it fresh. Ah ehn go say it any mo'

Hmmm, well if dis fish fresh den is I who dead an' gone
De ting smell like it take a bath in a lavatory in town
it here so long it happy. Look how de mout' laughin' at we
De eye turn up to heaven like it want tuh know 'e fate
Dey say it does take a good week before dey reach dat state

Yuh mango ripe?

Gran'ma, stop feelin' and squeezin' up meh fruit!
Yuh ehn playin' in no ban'. Meh mango eh no concertina

Ah tell yuh dis mango hard just like yuh face
One bite an' ah sure tuh break both ah meh plate
If yuh cahn tell de difference between green an' rosy red
dohn clim' jus' wait until dey fall down from de tree
Yuh go know dey ripe when de lizard and dem start tuh feed
but dohn bring yuh force-ripe fruit tuh try an' sell in here
it ehn burglars is crooks like all yuh poor people have to fear

De yam good?

Old lady, get yuh nails outta meh yam!
Ah mad tuh make yuh buy it now yuh damage it so bad

Dis yam look like de one dat did come off ah de ark
She brother in de Botanical Gardens up dey by Queens Park
Tourists with dey camera comin' from all over de worl'
takin' pictures dey never hear any yam could be dat ole
Ah have a crutch an' a rocking-chair someone give meh fuh free
If ah did know ah would ah bring dem an' leave dem here fuh she

De bush clean?

Well, I never hear more! Old woman, is watch yuh watching meh
young young dasheen leaf wit' de dew still shining on dem!

It seem tuh me like dey does like tuh lie out in de sun
jus' tuh make sure dat dey get dey edges nice an' brown
an' maybe is weight dey liftin' tuh make dem look so tough
Dey wan' build up dey strength fuh when tings start gettin' rough
Is callaloo ah makin' but ah 'fraid tings go get too hot
Yuh bush go want tuh fight an' meh crab go jump outta de pot

How much a poun' yuh fig?

Ah have a big big sign tellin' yuh how much it cos'
Yuh either blin' yuh dotish or yuh jus' cahn read at all

Well, ah wearing meh glasses so ah readin' yuh big big sign
but tuh tell yuh de trut' ah jus' cahn believe meh eye
Ah lookin' ah seein' but no man could be so blasted bol'
Yuh mus' tink dis is Fort Knox yuh sellin' fig as if is gol'
Dey should put all ah all yuh somewhere nice an' safe
If dey ehn close Sing-Sing prison dat go be the bestest place

De orange sweet?

Ma, it eh hah orange in dis market as sweet as ah does sell
It like de sun, it taste like sugar an' it juicy as well

Yuh know, boy, what yuh sayin' have a sorta ring
De las' time ah buy yuh tell meh exactly de same ting
When ah suck ah fin' all ah dem sour as hell
De dentures drop out an' meh two gum start tuh swell
Meh mout' so sore ah cahn even eat ah meal
Yuh sure it ehn lime all yuh wrappin' in orange peel?

De coconut hah water?

Sally-Ann Murray (b 1961)

Murray lives in Durban, where she teaches English at the University of Natal.
Her first collection of poems *Shifting* was joint winner of the 1991 Sanlam
Literary Award.

Under the freeway

little again
Our mother told us always – fragments on her mouth, her plate –
Eat up!
Don't play, she said –
For under the bridge were children cold and hungry.
What bridge? I mommyed her,
(half sass half sympathy)
Come take me?

(fearing always that she would).
In bed those nights the darkness
Overwhelmed.

Tonight, the *Tropicale* was festive.
Diffuse light, a tall carafe, and 'Bobby' –
Buttoned 'Waiter of the Week'.
But driving off:
A bogey vision now grown up,
Shapeless at first from the car's cocoon,
Seemed to launch towards the target.
No traffic, so we lurched ahead.
Behind us though, the bite of other brakes
As a squat stump figure
(Wary of speedsters beneath the flyover)
Bumped and scraped
His legless form
Down the gradient.

Read Dylan Thomas's poem 'Do not go gentle into that good night' (p. 72) for
an interesting comparison with this next poem.

For Poppa (1899–1983), DSM 1917

So this is it. Your struggle for survival –
Once fought against bullets, gas, hunger, mud – now shrunk
To a crocheted rug. Such thoughts aren't said, of course.
Anyway, you can't hear well; can't even tell
It's me. The rocker's slackening rhythm fills
The bedroom; blood-red at your feet, glowrock
Heaters throw ashy roses pale upon
Your nerve-thorned face. Bunched with dying. Crumpled
As never before, Nana nurses you.
Finds her place with phials, keeps to the pledge
For better or for worse, although she knows.
Somehow she carries on, knit one, slip one,
Making tea for two. No sad cries to sound
Its slow passing, the marriage circle narrows
To a clinically cortisoned zero.   *steroid used for inflammation*
Before I leave, in fact, before you go,   *and allergy*
One question: why are you fighting so to stay,
When everything is over, passed away?

Gabriela Pearse (b 1962)

Pearse was born in Bogota, Colombia, to a Trinidadian father and a British mother. After a childhood in the West Indies, she moved to the United Kingdom, and studied at Warwick University. She lives in London and works as a training consultant.

Today

A woman with a gash
so deep and wide in
her black soul
came and spilled her
self over me.

Asking to be held
like no-one held her

Asking to be fed
like no-one fed her.

She crawled beneath
my skirt trembling and
afraid and clasped
my lifeboat legs.

But I had meetings
to go to,
and a world to save.

Sarah Ruden (b 1963)

Ruden was born in the United States, but now lives in South Africa. She lectures in the Department of Classics at the University of Cape Town. She has a PhD from Harvard University. Her collection of poems *Other Places* won the 1996 CNA Literary Award. Religion is often a major concern in her poems.

The poet stares at a derelict on the street

If I lived with you
In the house of rain,
Would He come for me
When He comes again?

Would He buy me shoes
And show me where
To sleep? And spread
His jacket there?

If I lived with you,
Then I could see,
But now He will not
Come for me.

If I lived with you
In the house of rain,
Would He come for me
When He comes again?

The second coming

I went to see Him after the show.
He lay on a makeshift bed
In the trailer He used as a dressing room.
'I'm so confused,' He said.

'They *are* convinced – and the press is good –
But all they do is go home.'
He sighed and looked at His cigarette.
It went out on its own.

'I swear, if I see them one more time,
As they nod and gasp and smile,
Then gather their coats and find their keys
And pull their kids from the aisle,

'I'm gonna do that things with the Seals –
But that won't work, I know' –
A bottle of bourbon poured itself –
'They'll think it's part of the show.

'No wonder, of course: after all they've seen,
What is there that *I* can do?
You, for example' – He looked at me –
'How would I *begin*, with you?

'I would have quit this months ago,
  If not for the crew' – the bed
  Shook hard, and I dodged, as He drained His drink –
'It's a privilege to work with the dead.

'Tomorrow I'll feel like it's worth it again.
  The long term? I'll have to see.
  But I'd hate to drop all my favourite lines,
  Like "Come follow, come follow Me."'

Kristina Rungano (b 1963)

Rungano was born in rural Zimbabwe. After high school she studied computer science in the United Kingdom, and returned to Zimbabwe to work at the Scientific Computing Centre in Harare. She has published one collection of poems, *A Storm is Brewing*.

The woman

A minute ago I came from the well
Where young women drew water like myself
My body was weary and my heart tired.
For a moment I watched the stream that rushed before me;
And thought how fresh the smell of flowers,
How young the grass around it.
And yet again I heard the sound of duty
Which ground on me – made me feel aged
As I bore the great big mud container on my head
Like a great big painful umbrella.
Then I got home and cooked your meal
For you had been out drinking the pleasures of the flesh
While I toiled in the fields
Under the angry vigilance of the sun
A labour shared only by the bearings of my womb.
I washed the dishes – yours –
And swept the room we shared
Before I set forth to prepare your bedding
In the finest corner of the hut
Which was bathed by the sweet smell of dung
I had this morning applied to the floors
Then you came in,

In your drunken lust
And you made your demands
When I explained how I was tired
And how I feared for the child – yours – I carried
You beat me and had your way
At that moment
You left me unhappy and bitter
And I hated you;
Yet tomorrow I shall again wake up to you
Milk the cow, plough the land and cook your food,
You shall again be my Lord
For isn't it right that woman should obey,
Love, serve and honour her man?
For are you not fruit of the land?

Heather Robertson (b 1964)

Robertson was born in the Cape and studied at the University of Natal. She taught for a while in Cape Town, and has worked as a journalist. She has published one collection of her poems, *Under the Sun*.

There's a boy

there's a boy somewhere
up where the Tugela tames its tumble
and mealies green the land
he's there
in the days that wade blue and wide
a river brown reed
so slim and serene
he could snap in my teeth
but
that's not my dream
no
all i want is to watch him there
easing his leafy limbs
in each ripple of river and land

all i want
is to catch by chance

some rustling reed-talk
in my palms

and perhaps
perhaps if he sees me
perhaps if he dreams me
to swing
to the song
of his skin
for a while

Lesego Rampolokeng (b 1965)

Rampolokeng was born in Orlando West, Soweto, and studied at the University of the North. He is South Africa's foremost rap poet. Two collections of his poems have been published, *Horns for Hondo* and *Talking Rain*, and a cassette has been released of him performing his work, *End Beginnings*.

Rap and British dub poetry have once again placed rhyme centre-stage. Note how Rampolokeng uses internal rhyme as well as end-rhyme, for example the rhyme between 'late' and 'hate' in line 5 is an internal rhyme, and there is an '-ate' end-rhyme that runs from line 4 to line 8.

History

revolution or evolution
the game is still the same
reconciliation negotiation
it won't take the bait
it's too late for hate
when fate is your only mate
wipe the slate
you can't dictate history's date
BLACK on the attack
won't turn back
or slack
It's GREEN
going on mean
marching on the obscene
as in ho chi minh
if you know what i mean
marching on bold

it's GOLD unsold
the story untold
whose history turns time cold
when the murder mystery begins to unfold
it won't lace up the truth with arsenic
& claim to be platonic
& defecate when it denigrates
or swiss bank emigrate
accounting for the cost
cost of lives lost to buy glasnost
for the taxation of a nation
in the tradition of predation
between the breed of need
& the creed of greed
who mythify the truth
to mystify the path
we have to tread for bread to feed our seed

it goes on forever
it's sung by lips & tongues untied
for being strong not wrong
its rung is not cowdung
from civilization to annexation
with the intonation of damnation
from pit to hill from hell to heaven
perverted minds inverting triple seven
ah yell to tell how the L for LOVE fell

the bible on your table
& the manure in your stable
all misery no nursery rhymes
all files & all piles
of money to spend
with no fun in the sun but the gloat
of a trench coat
balance me without respite
& i'll give you insight
into both left & right
so you can fly your kite
in history's daylight

In the morning

the sun an upturned bowl spilling dark into
the opened palms of my morning window i look
out on a man sweeping fear that oozes out
of the pores of the street into a dustbin.
i look out. my days are the soot of yesterday's
smoke that spiralled to heaven in the fires that raged.
in the morning i look out on the litter of these
times. unwilling sacrificial lambs
that appease the hunger of a cannibal god.
i look out on vultures pecking their souls fleshless.

Sandile Dikeni (b 1966)

Dikeni was born in Victoria West, and educated in the Eastern Cape and at the
University of the Western Cape. In 1986, while he was a student leader, he was
detained for his political involvement. It was then that he began writing poetry.
He became well known as a performance poet at political rallies and community
cultural events. He has worked as a journalist in both the print and electronic
media in the Western Cape and in Gauteng. A collection of his poems has been
published, *Guava Juice*.

Love poem for my country

My country is for love
so say its valleys
where ancient rivers flow
the full circle of life
under the proud eye of birds
adorning the sky

My country is for peace
so says the veld
where reptiles caress
its surface
with elegant motions
glittering in their pride

My country
is for joy
so talk the mountains

with baboons
hopping from boulder to boulder
in the majestic delight
of cliffs and peaks

My country
is for health and wealth
see the blue of the sea
and beneath
the jewels of fish
deep under the bowels of soil
hear
the golden voice
of a miner's praise
for my country

My country
is for unity
feel the millions
see their passion
their hands are joined together
there is hope in their eyes

we shall celebrate

In the next poem the sections of songs and chants in Xhosa and the English
versions that follow them are to be spoken with a deliberate train-rhythm.

Track of the tracks

(for my brother Dicey who died of TB at the railways)

it begins
with a laugh
hard,
breathless as steel

Xhegwazana phek'ipapa
Xhegwazana phek'ipapa
Sayithath'apha
Sayibek'apha

Sayithath'apha
Sayibek'apha

Mama makes porridge
my granny makes porridge
take it here
put it there
take it here
put it there

there
the night comes sweating
perspiring outwards
drags the guts
in a blood red pulp
that drains the sweet
of youth
out
out to the harshness
of world
that leaves you cold
when sun
unveils generous blanket of light
but never touches
the inside of bone
and marrow shrivels
ice stone
inside
outside
inside the railway tracks
where we chant:

Sojikel'emaweni
emaweni
sojikel'emaweni
emaweni
sojikela'aphi na he?
he wee!
sojikela'aphi na he?
he wee!

We bend the cliffs
the cliffs

we bend the cliffs
the cliffs
we bend them for you
and you
hey you!

our breath is hot
like the hiss of Makadas
the steam train that puffs
against the winter wall
of a karoo drought
that bends, swerves
through our lives
black as the soot
from the coal mines of Newcastle
where some more black blood coughs
from deep down:
sishov'ingolovane
ngolovane
sishov'ingolovane
ngolovane

we push the small coal trains
against the winter's white breath
that cracks
under our boots
melts into ice crystals
hardens in our lungs' lobes
but we shall sing
warm longings:
Sdudla sibomvu
mathangan'abomvu
Sdudla sibomvu
mathangan'abomvu

my baby's hot
her thighs are red
my baby's hot
her thighs are red

sing, sing
until death comes,
sings,
in our breath.

Rustum Kozain (b 1966)

Kozain was born in Paarl in the Western Cape. He was educated at the University of Cape Town, where he won the Nelson Mandela Prize for Poetry in 1988. He was a Fullbright Scholar to the United States in 1994–95. He is now busy on his doctorate in English.

At the feet of a child

for Emma Maria 1995–

The earth is young again tonight
And innocent of dinosaurs

Of war and famine; and small,
Cauled underneath a child:

Seven months, Emma rocks
On all small fours and belly

Rocks back and forth
Until her feet find traction

And, gurgling, she launches
Into her first crawl, sets us

And the earth in motion

Brother, who will bury me?

1

   If I stand long enough on Paarl Rock
On my toes in the cold in only jeans
And a t-shirt fluttering about my torso
As if I've just jumped from heaven,
Maybe I'll dream of *Maalik-il-Mout*,
The Angel of Death in red and white
Who comes not only for the soul
But, piercing rakish fingers all at once
Into nostrils, eye-sockets and throat, plucks
The life from you in one twist-draw-and-clasp.
Then, wordlessly looking to the heavens
He leaps with one more soul bound for God.

Brother, who will then bury me, and where?
Prepared for Muslim burial, slender corpse
Hidden under a sheet spanned by several hands
While men in gleaming foreheads and solemn beards
Avoid each other's eyes, muttering prayers
Furtive as their hands that lift and touch to wash.

By chance, will one washer see where I've scarred
My body, unhappy with the Lord's image;
Where I've a tattoo of a crescent and star?
Will he fall silent, murmur prayers for my redemption
Or alert the others? Will they abandon
My body, outraged that in death too I come
To shame and mock my father? Or forgive me?

Bagged in linen, draped under a green spread
Will I be carried in a stumble
Of obligation, my bier exchanged often
So everyone may find grace, rewards
From their duty while rushing me to the grave
In a two mile hike through gawking streets?

If I should be lifted by childhood friends
Now all grown unequal in height, and the bier cants
And I slip out like a mutter, awkward as my birth,
An interruption in the ceremonial march,
Will they fumble to hoist me in haste
The disgrace of my corpse on tarmac quickly
Overcome, as soon too the earth will ingest me?
Earth that waits under cold bluegum and pine tree
On the small incline of Paarl's cemetery
Reserved with pockmarked crescent and star
Riding at odd-angles the wire-mesh gate
And cut unevenly from tin, in agitprop haste
As death and burials here are, something
To get over with? Here, where three feet of loam betrays
My universe of yellow-red, dank clay; my berth
At six feet, a wedge-shaped niche at the bottom,
A crawlspace dug facing north-north-east?

Will three men pounce into the hole, unmoved
By the damp soil clotting on their clothes,
And reach to me as others drape the green pall

Over the grave, funeral-goers glimpsing
Only earth-caked hands, dark loam, clay bed, mummy?

          Unmechanical, I will slump
Like a sodden cocoon into the arms
And cracked palms of artisans, my brothers
Who will puff and stamp and mumble directions
Under the green tent; men who will lay me
Down rough on my right side, facing Mecca
Where *Ibrahim* first praised God and built the *Kaaba*,
A hovering stone his faithful scaffold
That now, polished by millions of pilgrims'
Hands, stares at them like a giant fish-eye.

   Above-ground, someone will mix soil
And water, and will hand the bucket down.
And others will pass on planks, inches thick;
Others, plucked branches from the bluegum trees,
Lush, with thin, long leaves: our substitute
For olive. While the air will swell with chants,
Pleas to God to take me into heaven
Three men will rush to cover me in leaves,
Slant planks across my niche, and seal me up
                    with mortar.

   Now things will move quickly: the last man
Hardly hoisted out, but spadefuls of dirt cough
Over my crypt. God's earth weighing in.
No one allowed to tire, spades change rapid
Hands that rush my story to its end. Now

   Brothers in Islam, of my early faith
Go and rest with your share of grief, of duty.
You redeem those who failed to carry my bier,
Handle my corpse, pass on mortar, timber, leaf.
All free from this duty, as all would be
Had only one buried me. Our God is merciful.
                    Now go

   To my parents' house and briefly mourn my death.
Share with those who travelled far to pay respects
Share with them a plate of food, sugar-bean stew
With gravy thick and red as mud, and hope

My father could afford small chunks of beef,
That the *dhanya* was fresh, fresh from this earth
This *dhunya*, this world that I now leave.
Dip your hands into mounds of *basmati*
Catch some gravy in the funnel of your fingers
And think of me. I, who for years feasted
On ham and wine, I still burn, died burning
For a mound of *basmati* and sugar-beans.

*

Buried in the quick of Islamic death,
I won't be mourned for long, but several moments.
And seven days later, when you gather again
To remember my death, I'll be far gone;
Forty nights later, one hundred nights later,
All your chants billowing me along,
Consider then my slow journey that starts only now:

When the last person leaves and his foot lifts
Forty paces away, *Azrafeel* will twirl
From limbo and bring me his terror
Of questions. Mace at the ready, he is
My first officer of inquisition
And he'll pore over the catalogues of my deeds
Kept by *Israeel* and *Ismaeel*, and weigh the book
Of my left shoulder against that of my right.

And, forty steps away, who will hear me shriek
As *Azrafeel* swings mace, twists my eyes out
Rips my tongue to shreds with heavenly nails
Grips my groin so I may admit to my sins?
Who will think of my torture, earnestly
Pray, brother, for the angel's mercy here
At the start, only the start, of my final journey?

In the neighbourhood, I know cats and dogs
Will howl, trees bend north-north-east in witness.
Close to God, they know my terror. But
Elsewhere, in other countries, other towns,
Will birds' wings spring into sharp chatter,
Will moles coil with doubt in their burrows,
Ants shrivel to death as if in hot air?

Will the gecko's pulse build until
Its blood stops and, stalling, we are one?

2

Or no? No…

Abandoned, will my body ponder its life
Thrown hugely against a white-tiled morgue
Where orderlies conduct the day over me,
My eyeballs roaming the domes of their lids
As, new to religion, a child wonders
At the concave inside of a minaret?

Slowly, I'll grow to inhabit decay
Counting years by the stolid pauses of blood.
The swell of bloat won't perturb the orderly.
He has seen it all and will sign some forms
On behalf of the deceased carted off by science
Slipping from the swing-bottom of a poorman's box.

3

Yes. I'll die homeless. And grow quiet
As the earth; buried in the pauper's graveyard
In Paarl, where the unknown and the wretched lie
In a rusty field, next to the meadow
Where horses stare at their future as petfood;
Close to where, after a fight with my brother,
To heal the hurt that he was bigger, stronger,
That I could never win, with strength or reason,
I walked to heal that heartbreak. Ten, I walked

Into the veld, sat next to a small river
That reeked of laundry and decay from upstream
Where the poor washed clothes and everything else.
In a bleached Coke can, I stuck a malaise
Of veldflowers, took them home to my mother
And cried, sobbed in frustration, unable
To show her the solace in knowing
One's alone, even as that solace hurt more.

*

Decades ago this graveyard was a jumble
Of shacks. Migrant workers, their wives and children
All without Passes, lived here, called it
Bongweni, favourite place. Shacks long razed, people
Evicted, some caught crouching still in rock
Like fossil waiting to spring into beginning
Here in this favourite place with its rows of graves;

Here,

I want to lie here.
                    And feel other children
Tug at veldflowers, rip solace from sods
And even if their palms should bleed, offer
My death to tearful, comforting mothers.

Seitlhamo Motsapi (b 1966)

Motsapi was born in Bela-Bela, Warmbaths, and has been a teacher and
university lecturer. A collection of his poems has been published, *earthstepper/
the ocean is very shallow.*

the man

an almost forgotten acquaintance
was in town recently
i noticed that it started raining
just as he ambled in

i remember him as a simple man
growing up,we all wanted
to be doctors,lawyers & teachers
so the blood could ebb out of the village

my friend had much more sober dreams
he asked the heavens to grant him
the imposing peace of the blue-gum in his backyard
& that all the poor send him their tears
so he could be humble like the sun
so the red wax of the stars would not drip onto him

i remembered that man today
& all i think of is his unassuming radiance
like that of a blushing angel

as for his dreams
he tells us
whole forests invade his sleep at night
so that there's only standing room
for the dreams

Lemn Sissay (b 1968)

Sissay was born in Billinge in the United Kingdom. He says, 'I am British, of course I'm British. But being British and black are two different things … the system here doesn't accept the Britishness of Blacks.' Two collections of his have been published: *Perceptions of the Pen* and *Tender Fingers in a Clenched Fist*. He is a regular performer of his work and has performed his poems in South Africa.

Spell me freedom

Spell me freedom
And make it simple
So when I eat
It shall not make me sick

Spell me freedom
And make the ingredients carefully
So when I drink
It does not make me choke

Spell me freedom
And whisper it quietly
So when we speak
It does not give me a headache

Spell me freedom
And bake it fresh
So when I'm thirsty
It shall not make me dry

Spell me freedom
And stir it quickly
So when I taste
It shall not burn my tongue

Spell me freedom
And tell the joke well
So that when I laugh
It shall not unveil into hopeless tears

Spell me freedom
and cradle each word
That when I use them
They shall not crack like spines

Adam Schwartzman (b 1973)

Schwartzman was born and educated in Johannesburg. After a year of teaching and travel, he entered Pembroke College, Oxford. His first collection of poems has been published, *The Good Life. The Dirty Life. and other stories.*

Rivonia Road 2

without words

Crouching on the roof of your neighbour's garage that slopes
over the garden and your mother's rosery, we watch a squall
drub and clobber the Magaliesberg foothills from far away.

In the suburbs though, it is a dumb-show. We count
the long seconds between flash and wallop and try
to remember the formula to link sight and sound by distance.

What we see is the storm, small and entire in the wide sky and neatly
defined between two tilted parallels. As they open up nearer,
we will smell them cleanly. We will see through rain-shade.

Things will be darker, not dimmer. When it comes to us,
we will be inside, safely, until, afterwards, we clear the garden table
and find the wine-glasses brimmed and level.

The leaving

Children found the body,
naked as a god
and washed up on the beach.
Neap tide brought us
the young man,
catch of the day, splayed
in an X, making angel shapes.

I would like to have known him,
though not to stop him.
I hope he spoke softly
or not at all, leaning
on the railings by the pier
watching the swell rise and fall
into troughs and rise

and fall again. Freshly dead,
not yet spoiled, and the sea
will flow forever
through the neat holes
in his head. You could really believe
it was only to be part
of everything he loved.

Acknowledgements

The editor and publishers gratefully acknowledge permission to reproduce copyright poems in this book. Every effort has been made to trace copyright holders, but where this has proved impossible, the publishers would be grateful for information which would enable them to amend any omissions in future editions. In the information below, all titles of books for which no author is given, are authored by the poet.

Lionel Abrahams: 'Celebration' from *A Dead Tree Full of Live Birds*, reprinted by permission of Snailpress and Hippogriff Press. 'The whiteman blues' from *Thresholds of Tolerance*, reprinted by permission of Bateleur Press.

Chinua Achebe: 'Lazarus' and 'Refugee mother and child' from *Beware Soul Brother* published by Heinemann.

Tatamkhulu Afrika: 'The beggar' from *Maqabane* published by Mayibuye Books. 'The prisoner' from *Nine Lives* published by Carrefour Press. Both reprinted by permission of the author.

John Agard: 'Half-caste' and 'Rainbow' reprinted by kind permission of John Agard c/o Caroline Sheldon Literary Agency. Both poems from *Get Back Pimple* published by Viking 1996.

Ama Ata Aidoo: 'From the only speech that was not delivered at the rally' from *Someone Talking to Sometime* published by College Press, Harare, Zimbabwe. Reprinted by permission of the author.

Maya Angelou: 'Old folks laugh' from the book *I Shall not be Moved* by Maya Angelou, published by Virago Press. 'On aging' from the book *And Still I Rise* by Maya Angelou, published by Virago Press. 'They went home' from the book *Just Give Me a Cool Drink* by Maya Angelou, published by Virago Press.

Farouk Asvat: 'Possibilities for a man hunted by SBs' from *The Time of our Lives* published by Black Thoughts Publications. Reprinted by permission of the author.

Margaret Atwood: 'Woman skating' from *Procedures for Underground* by Margaret Atwood. Copyright © Oxford University Press Canada 1970. Reprinted by permission of Oxford University Press Canada.

W H Auden: 'Funeral blues' and 'Musée des Beaux Arts' from *Collected Poems* published by Faber and Faber Ltd.

James Baldwin: 'Song (for Skip) section 2' from *Jimmy's Blues* © 1983 by James Baldwin. Reprinted by arrangement with the James Baldwin Estate.

Shabbir Banoobhai: 'by your own definition' and 'you cannot know the fears i have' from *Shadows of a Sun-darkened Land* published by Ravan Press (Pty) Ltd. '*From Iqbal it is winter here still*' from *Echoes of my Other Self* published by Ravan Press (Pty) Ltd. Both reprinted by permission of the author.

James Berry: 'White child meets black man' from *Fractured Circles* published by New Beacon Books, 1979.

Earle Birney: 'Meeting of strangers' from *The Collected Poems: Earle Birney* by Earle Birney. Used by permission of McClelland & Stewart, Inc., Toronto, *The Canadian Publishers*.

Elizabeth Bishop: 'First death in Nova Scotia' and 'Seascape' from *The Complete Poems 1927–1979* by Elizabeth Bishop. Copyright © 1984 by Alice Helen Methfessel. Reprinted by permission of Farrar, Strauss and Giroux, Inc.

Gwendolyn Brooks: 'The bean eaters' from *The Bean Eaters* published by Harper and Row. 'To be in love' from *Selected Poems* published by Harper and Row.

Dennis Brutus: 'Letters to Martha 4', 'Letters to Martha 9' and 'Letters to Martha 10' from *A Simple Lust* published by Heinemann.

Roy Campbell: 'On some South African novelists' and 'On the same' from *Selected Poems*. Reprinted by permission of Francisco Campbell Custodio and Ad Donker Publishers.

John Pepper Clark-Bekederemo: 'Ibadan' and 'Night rain' from *A Decade of Tongues* published by Longman.

Lucille Clifton: 'Miss Rosie' copyright © 1986 by Lucille Clifton. Reprinted from *Good Woman: Poems and a Memoir 1969–1980* by Lucille Clifton, with the permission of BOA Editions, Ltd, Rochester, New York, USA.

Sydney Clouts: 'Karroo stop' from *Collected Poems*, reprinted by permission of David Philip Publishers.

Wendy Cope: 'Another Christmas poem', 'Bloody men' and 'Serious concerns' from *Serious Concerns* published by Faber and Faber Ltd.

Jeni Couzyn: 'Dilemma of a telephone operator' from *Christmas in Africa* published by Heinemann. Thanks to Jeni Couzyn © Jeni Couzyn 1975. 'In the house of the father' from *Life by Drowning: Selected Poems*. Thanks to Jeni Couzyn and Bloodaxe Publications.

Jeremy Cronin: 'Faraway city, there', 'I saw your mother' and 'Visiting room' from *Inside* published by Ravan Press (Pty) Ltd.

Patrick Cullinan: 'The beach, the evening' and 'The first, far beat' from *Selected Poems 1961–1994* published by Snailpress.

E E Cummings: 'i thank You God for most this amazing', 'in Just-' and 'my sweet old etcetera' are reprinted from *Complete Poems 1904–1962* by E E Cummings, edited by George J Firmage, by permission of W W Norton and Company. Copyright © 1991 by the Trustees for the E E Cummings Trust and George James Firmage.

Achmat Dangor: 'Paradise' from *Bulldozer* published by Ravan Press (Pty) Ltd.

Jennifer Davids: 'Poem for my mother' from *Searching for Words*, reprinted by permission of the author and David Philip Publishers.

C Day Lewis: 'Come, live with me and be my love' and 'Walking away' from *The Complete Poems* by C Day Lewis, published by Sinclair-Stevenson (1992). Copyright © 1992 in this edition The Estate of C Day Lewis.

Robert Dederick: 'Mantis' from *Bi-focal*, reprinted by permission of the author and David Philip Publishers.

Ingrid de Kok: 'Safe delivery' from *Carapace* magazine Vol 1, No 4. 'Small passing' from *Familiar Ground* published by Ravan Press (Pty) Ltd.

Eunice de Souza: 'De Souza Prabhu' from *Faber Book of Vernacular Verse* edited by Tom Paulin, published by Faber and Faber Ltd. Copyright Eunice de Souza.

Anthony Delius: 'The gamblers' and 'Emerald dove' from *A Corner of the World* published by Human and Rousseau.

Sandile Dikeni: 'Love poem for my country' from *Guava Juice* published by Mayibuye Books. 'Track of the tracks' from *New Contrast* No 88. Both reprinted by permission of the author.

Modikwe Dikobe: 'Grave of unknown whiteman' from *Dispossessed* published by Ravan Press (Pty) Ltd.

C J Driver: 'Grace and Silence' and 'Well, goodbye' from *In the Water-margins* published by Snailpress. Both reprinted by permission of the author.

Carol Ann Duffy: 'Foreign' from *Selling Manhattan* by Carol Ann Duffy, published by Anvil Press Poetry, 1987. 'In Mrs Tilscher's class' from *The Other Country* by Carol Ann Duffy, published by Anvil Press Poetry, 1990.

T S Eliot: 'The hollow men', 'Journey of the Magi' and 'Preludes' from *Collected Poems 1909–1962* published by Faber and Faber Ltd.

Nissim Ezekiel: 'The patriot' from *Latter-Day Psalms* published by Oxford University Press India, 1982.

U A Fanthorpe: 'You will be hearing from us shortly' copyright U A Fanthorpe, from *Standing To* (1982), reproduced by permission of Peterloo Poets.

Barry Feinberg: 'No cause for alarm' from *Gardens of Struggle* published by Mayibuye Books. Reprinted by permission of the author.

James Fenton: 'Cambodia' from *The Memory of War and Children in Exile* published by Penguin Books. 'Hinterhof' from *Penguin Modern Poets 1* edited by Fenton, Morrison and Wright, published by Penguin Books. Both reprinted by permission of the Peters Fraser and Dunlop Group Ltd.

Lawrence Ferlinghetti: 'Constantly risking absurdity' from *A Coney Island of the Mind* published by Bloodaxe Publications. Reprinted by permission of New Directions Publishing Corporation.

Nigel Fogg: 'Magnolia Clinic' from *English Alive 1968* published by SACEE. Reprinted by permission of the author.

Robert Frost: 'Mending wall' and 'Out, out –' from *The Poetry of Robert Frost* edited by Edward Connery Lathem, published by Henry Holt and Co., Inc. 'Stopping by woods on a snowy evening' from *The Poetry of Robert Frost* edited by Edward Connery Lathem, published by Henry Holt and Co., Inc. Copyright © 1923, 1969 by Henry Holt and Co., copyright © 1951 by Robert Frost. Reprinted by permission of Henry Holt and Co., Inc.

Zulfikar Ghose: 'The loss of India' © 1964 by Zulfikar Ghose, first published in *The Loss of India* published by Routledge and Kegan Paul, London. 'The picnic in Jammu' © 1967 by Zulfikar Ghose, first published in *Jets from Orange* published by Macmillan, London. 'Decomposition' © 1967 by Zulfikar Ghose, first published in *Jets from Orange* published by Macmillan, London.

Nikki Giovanni: 'Knoxville, Tennessee' from *Black Judgement* published by Broadside Press. © 1968 Nikki Giovanni. 'Nikki Rosa' from *Black Feeling Black Talk* published by William Morrow and Co. © 1968 Nikki Giovanni.

Thom Gunn: 'On the move' from *The Sense of Movement* published by Faber and Faber Ltd.

Mafika Pascal Gwala: 'Kwela-ride' and 'One small boy longs for summer' from *Jol'iinkomo*, reprinted by permission of the author and Ad Donker Publishers.

Caroline Halliday: 'ode to my daughter's plimsolls…' from *The New British Poetry 1968–88* edited by Gillian Allnut et al, published by Paladin Grafton Books Collins.

Shakuntala Hawoldar: 'Destruction' and 'To my little girl' from *Heinemann Book of African Women's Poetry* edited by S and F Chipasula, published by Heinemann.

Seamus Heaney: 'Digging', 'Follower' and 'Station Island section vii' from *New Selected Poems 1966–1987* published by Faber and Faber Ltd.

David Holbrook: 'Fingers in the door' from *Imaginings* published by Putnam and Co.

Amelia Blossom House: 'I will still sing' reprinted from *Our Sun Will Rise: Poems for South Africa* by Amelia Blossom House. Copyright © 1989 by Amelia Blossom House. Used with permission of Lynne Rienner Publishers, Inc.

Chenjerai Hove: 'A war-torn wife' from *Up in Arms* published by Zimbabwe Publishing House. 'You will forget' from *The Red Hills of Home* published by Mambo Press.

Langston Hughes: 'Life is fine' and 'Madam and the rent man' from *The Collected Poems of Langston Hughes* published by Vintage (US).

Ted Hughes: 'Chaucer' and 'The thought-fox' from *New Selected Poems 1957–1994* published by Faber and Faber Ltd.

Elizabeth Jennings: 'For a child born dead' and 'One flesh' from *Collected Poems* published by Carcanet Press Ltd.

Fhazel Johennesse: 'the night train', 'the nightwatchman' and 'a young man's thoughts before june the 16th' from *The Rainmaker* published by Ravan Press (Pty) Ltd.

Amryl Johnson: 'Granny in de market place' from *Long Road to Nowhere* published by Cofa Press, 1992.

Linton Kwesi Johnson: 'Mekkin histri' from *Tings an Times* published by Bloodaxe Publications.

Jenny Joseph: 'Warning' from *New Poems 1965* published by Hutchinson and Co.

Bernard Kops: 'Shalom bomb' from *Erica I Want to Read You Something* published by Scorpion Press.

Rustum Kozain: 'At the feet of a child' and 'Brother, who will bury me?' reprinted by permission of the author.

Mazisi Kunene: 'Congregation of the story-tellers . . .' from *The Ancestors and the Sacred Mountain* published by Heinemann.

Ben J Langa: 'For my brothers (Mandla and Bheki) in exile' from *Staffrider* Feb 1980 published by Ravan Press (Pty) Ltd. Reprinted with the permission of The Estate of Ben J Langa.

Philip Larkin: 'Ambulances' from *Collected Poems* published by Faber and Faber. 'Church going', 'Lines on a young lady's photograph album' and 'Coming' are reprinted from *The Less Deceived*, by permission of the Marvell Press, England and Australia.

Denise Levertov: 'The peachtree' and 'The secret' from *Poems 1960–1967* published by Bloodaxe Books. Reprinted by permission of New Directions Publishing Corporation.

Douglas Livingstone: 'Blue stuff' and 'Gentling a wildcat' from *Selected Poems*, reprinted by permission of the author and Ad Donker Publishers. 'Scourings at Station 19' from *A Littoral Zone* published by Carrefour Press.

Moira Lovell: 'Repossession' and 'Suburban intruder' from *Out of the Mist* published by Snailpress.

Robert Lowell: 'Terminal days at Beverly Farms' from *Life Studies* published by Faber and Faber Ltd. 'Women, children, babies, cows, cats' from *History* published by Faber and Faber Ltd.

Marjorie Oludhe Macgoye: 'A freedom song' from *Song of Nyarloka and Other Poems* published by Oxford University Press, Nairobi.

Louis MacNeice: 'Prayer before birth' from *Collected Poems* published by Faber and Faber Ltd.

Chris Zithulele Mann: 'Epiphanies' from *Kites* published by David Philip Publishers. 'To Lucky with his guitar…' from *New Shades* published by David Philip Publishers. Both reprinted by permission of the author and David Philip Publishers. 'The homecoming' from *South Africans: A Set of Portrait Poems*, Pietermaritzburg: University of Natal Press, 1996. 'In praise of the shades' from *First Poems*, by permission of the author and Bateleur Press.

Jack Mapanje: 'Your tears still burn at my handcuffs (1991)' from *The Chattering Wagtails of Mikuyu Prison* published by Heinemann Educational Publishers. © Jack Mapanje 1993.

Don Mattera: 'Let the children decide' and 'Remember' from *Azanian Love Song* published by Justified Press.

James Matthews: 'the face of my mother takes the shape' from *No Time for Dreams* published by Blac Publishing House.

Gcina Mhlophe: 'The dancer' from *Breaking the Silence* edited by Cecily Lockett, published by Ad Donker. 'Sometimes when it rains' from *Sometimes When It Rains* edited by Ann Oosthuizen, published by Pandora Press, Routledge Kegan and Paul Ltd.

Ruth Miller: 'It is better to be together' and 'Mantis' from *Poems Prose Plays* edited by Lionel Abrahams, by permission of Carrefour Press and Lionel Abrahams representing Pat Campbell.

Stan Motjuwadi: 'Taken for a ride' from *To Whom It May Concern* edited by Robert Royston, published by Ad Donker.

Seitlhamo Motsapi: 'the man' from *earthstepper/the ocean is very shallow* published by Deep South Publishing, Box 2482, Cape Town 8000.

Mbuyiseni Oswald Mtshali: 'An abandoned bundle' from *Sounds of a Cowhide Drum*, 1982. By permission of Oxford University Press, Oxford.

Micere Githae Mugo: 'Where are those songs?' from *Daughter of My People Sing* (pp2–4) by Micere Githae Mugo, published by the East African Literature Bureau, 1976.

Charles Mungoshi: 'If you don't stay bitter for too long' and 'Sitting on the balcony' from *Zimbabwean Poetry in English* edited by K Z Muchemwa, published by Mambo Press.

Sally-Ann Murray: 'For Poppa (1899-1983), DSM 1917' and 'Under the freeway' from *Shifting* in *Signs*, by permission of Carrefour Press and the author.

Grace Nichols: 'Praise song for my mother' from the book *The Fat Black Woman's Poems* by Grace Nichols, published by Virago Press. Permission granted by the publishers, Karnack House, for the poem 'In my name' extracted from the collection *I is a long memoried Woman* by Grace Nichols. © 1983/1996 Karnack House.

Mike Nicol: 'New men' from *Among the Souvenirs* published by Ravan Press (Pty) Ltd.

Gabriel Okara: 'One night at Victoria Beach' and 'You laughed and laughed and laughed' from *The Fisherman's Invocation* published by Heinemann Educational Publishers. © Gabriel Okara 1978.

Christopher Okigbo: 'Come thunder' from *Collected Poems* published by Heinemann Educational Nigeria Ltd. © Estate of Christopher Okigbo 1986.

Ben Okri: 'You walked gently towards me' from *An African Elegy* published by Jonathan Cape.

Oodgeroo of the tribe Noonuccal (formerly known as Kath Walker): 'Last of his tribe' and 'Acacia Ridge' from *My People, Third edition*, 1990, published by Jacaranda Press.

Niyi Osundare: 'The poet' from *Selected Poems* published by Heinemann Educational Publishers. © Niyi Osundare 1992.

Donald Parenzee: 'Feeding' and 'Then the children decided' from *Driven to Work* published by Ravan Press (Pty) Ltd.

Alan Paton: 'To a small boy who died at Diepkloof Reformatory' from *Knocking on the Door*, reprinted by permisson of David Philip Publishers.

Gabriela Pearse: 'Today' from *Daughters of Africa* edited by Margaret Busby, published by Jonathan Cape.

Lenrie Peters: 'Parachute men say' from *Satellites* published by Heinemann Educational Publishers. © Lenrie Peters 1967.

Marie Philip: 'Black dog' from *Contrast* No 29 1972, reprinted by permission of the author.

Sylvia Plath: 'The arrival of the bee box', 'Daddy', 'Tulips' and 'You're' from *Collected Poems* published by Faber and Faber Ltd.

William Plomer: 'The taste of the fruit' from *Collected Poems* published by Jonathan Cape. By permission of The Estate of William Plomer.

Karen Press: 'Clever man', 'Not forgetting' and 'When your child is born, mother' from *Bird Heart Stoning the Sea* published by Buchu Books. © Karen Press.

Taufiq Rafat: 'Circumcision' has been reproduced from *Wordfall* (Oxford University Press, Pakistan, 1975) by kind permission of the author. 'The squalor in which some people live' has been reproduced from *Pieces of Eight* (Oxford University Press, Pakistan, 1975) by kind permission of the author.

Lesego Rampolokeng: 'History' from *Talking Rain* published by COSAW. 'In the morning' from *Horns for Hondo* published by COSAW.

Adrienne Rich: 'Song' from *Diving into the Wreck: Poems 1971–1972* by Adrienne Rich. Copyright © 1973 by W W Norton and Company, Inc. Reprinted by permission of the author and W W Norton and Company, Inc.

Heather Robertson: 'There's a boy' from *Under the Sun* published by Snailpress, 1991.

Judith Rodriguez: 'How come the truck-loads?' from *Judith Rodriguez: New and Selected Poems* published by the University of Queensland Press, 1988.

Heather Royes: 'Theophilus Jones walks naked down King Street' from *An Anthology of African and Caribbean Writing in English* edited by John Figueroa, published by Heinemann Educational Publishers.

Sarah Ruden: 'The poet stares at a derelict on the street' and 'The second coming' in *Other Places* first published by Justified Press, now published by Jonathan Ball Publishers.

Kristina Rungano: 'The woman' from *A Storm is Brewing* published by Zimbabwe Publishing House.

Adam Schwartzmann: 'The leaving' and 'Rivonia Road 2' from *The Good Life. The Dirty Life. And Other Stories* published by Carcanet Press Ltd, 1995.

Helen Segal: 'Let's do away with the show' from *New South African Writing* Volume 5 published by Purnell (whose list C Struik has subsequently bought).

Magoleng wa Selepe: 'My name' from *Staffrider*, published by Ravan Press (Pty) Ltd.

Mongane Wally Serote: 'The actual dialogue', and 'Hell, well, heaven' from *Yakhal'inkomo*, reprinted by permission of Mongane Wally Serote and Ad Donker Publishers. 'For Don M. – banned' from *Tsetlo*, reprinted by permission of Mongane Wally Serote and Ad Donker Publishers.

Anne Sexton: 'Wanting to die' from *The Complete Poems* published by Houghton Mifflin Co. Reprinted by permission of Sterling Lord Literistic, Inc. Copyright © 1966 by Anne Sexton.

Ntozake Shange: 'Lady in red' from *Coloured Girls who have Considered Suicide* published by Methuen, London. © Ntozake Shange.

Lemn Sissay: 'Spell me freedom' from *Tender Fingers in a Clenched Fist* published by Bogle L'Ouverture Publications Ltd.

Adam Small: 'O kroeskop!' from *Kitaar my Kruis* published by Kagiso Publishers, formerly HAUM.

Mavis Smallberg: 'A small boy' from *Essential Things* edited by Andries Oliphant, published by COSAW. The poem is dedicated to 'all the small boys who gave up their childhood and who have become part of the so-called lost generation'.

Stevie Smith: 'Away, melancholy' and 'Not waving but drowning' from *The Collected Poems of Stevie Smith* by Stevie Smith (Penguin 20th Century Classics). Reprinted by permission of James MacGibbon, the executor of Smith's estate.

Kelwyn Sole: 'My countrymen' and 'Tiny victories' from *The Blood of our Silence* published by Ravan Press (Pty) Ltd.

Wole Soyinka: 'Telephone conversation' from *Three Thousand Years of Black Poetry: An Anthology* edited by Alan Lomax and Raoul Abdul, published by Dodd, Mead (New York). 'To the madmen over the wall' from *The Shuttle in the Crypt*, published by Rex Collings and Methuen.

Stephen Spender: 'My parents kept me from children who were rough' from *Collected Poems 1928–1985* published by Faber and Faber Ltd.

Anne Stevenson: 'Utah' and 'The victory' reprinted from Anne Stevenson's *Selected Poems 1956–1986* (1987) by permission of Oxford University Press.

May Swenson: 'The key to everything' from *The Love Poems of May Swenson*. Copyright © 1991 by The Literary Estate of May Swenson. Reprinted by permission of Houghton Mifflin Co. All rights reserved.

Dylan Thomas: 'Do not go gentle into that good night' and 'The hunchback in the park' from *The Poems* published by J M Dent. Copyright © Trustees for the copyrights of Dylan Thomas.

Christopher van Wyk: 'In detention', 'Injustice' and 'A riot policeman' from *It is Time to go Home* published by Ad Donker. By permission of the author.

Derek Walcott: 'The fist' from *Collected Poems 1948–1984* published by Faber and Faber Ltd. 'Lizard' (an excerpt from 'A Tropical Bestiary') from *Poems 1965–1980* published by Jonathan Cape. Copyright © 1964 Derek Walcott.

Alice Walker: 'The kiss' and extracts from 'Once' reprinted on pages 186 to 188 are from *Once* by Alice Walker, published in Great Britain by The Women's Press Ltd, 1986, 34 Great Sutton Street, London EC1V 0DX.

Stephen Watson: 'Commonplaces' from *Presence of the Earth*, reprinted by permission of the author and David Philip Publishers.

William Carlos Williams: 'The act', 'The artist' and 'This is just to say' from *Collected Poems* published by Carcanet Press Ltd.

Judith Wright: 'Flying-fox on barbed wire' and 'Request to a year' from *Collected Poems* published by HarperCollins Australia. Reprinted by permission of HarperCollins Publishers. 'Woman to man' from *A Human Pattern: Selected Poems* published by ETT Imprint, Watsons Bay 1996.

Benjamin Zephaniah: 'According to my mood' from *City Psalms* published by Bloodaxe Publications. © Benjamin Zephaniah.

Musaemura Zimunya: 'Cattle in the rain' and 'The reason' from *Thought Tracks* published by Addison Wesley Longman. Reprinted by permission of Addison Wesley Longman Ltd.

Index of titles

Index of authors